EAT THE DONKEY

WHY GREAT COMPANIES EMBRACE DISCOMFORT

ANTHONY REEVES

CONTENTS

ISBN: 979-8-9887424-5-6 (Paperback)

ISBN: 979-8-9887424-4-9 (Hardback)

ISBN: 979-8-9887424-6-3 (ebook)

Book cover design by MECOB Design.

Edited by Nathan Pettijohn.

Printed by Cordurouy LLC in the United States of America.

First printing edition 2026.

Cordurouy Books

704 Hermosa Ave

Hermosa Beach, CA 90254

www.cordurouy.com

PRAISE FOR EAT THE DONKEY

"The courage to be uncomfortable—in print."

—**Karna Crawford**, former head of U.S. marketing, Ford Motor Company

"Anthony Reeves' *Eat the Donkey* is the kick in the ass every marketer and agency needs right now."

—**Rob Schwartz**, former CEO TBWA\Chiat\Day NY

"Disruptive technologies and rapidly shifting markets pose a dilemma for growing companies: tighten their grip on successful strategies or embrace a culture of change? Reeves makes a compelling case that continuing success demands both, and clearly shows us how it's done."

—**Tom Schonhoff**, employee #5 at Amazon

"There are two types of marketing professionals—those hiding behind ineffective 'best practices' and those willing to ask tough questions. Anthony Reeves belongs to the latter, turning his experiences into wisdom, making this an enjoyable and essential read for those navigating marketing's evolving landscape."

—**Ian Baer**, founder & CEO at Sooth

"First, forgive yourself for everything you learn you're doing wrong. Then, get a highlighter."
    —**Kat Gordon**, Founder/CEO of The 3% Movement

"Discomfort is the new competitive advantage."
    —**Walt Greer**, CCO of Innovation for North America, VML

ABOUT THE AUTHOR

Anthony Reeves helped transform global brands such as Amazon, Nike, Airbnb, Kohler, and LVMH through C-suite creative and strategy roles, helping Fortune 500 companies break free from the comfortable stagnation that kills growth. A three-time Cannes Lions keynote speaker, with appearances in NYT and Forbes, and Campaign of the Year winner, he bridges creative excellence with business transformation at companies ranging from tech giants to century-old enterprises. Anthony has stood on international podiums as an Ironman and long-course triathlete, and as an ultra-events participant. He believes that lasting success—in boardrooms or endurance sports—requires deliberately choosing productive discomfort over the hubris and comfort of decline. He lives in Wisconsin with his family.

anthonyreeves.co
@anthony.j.reeves

INTRODUCTION

The Expedition

I was seven years old, wedged between siblings on a sweaty vinyl back row of a dust-caked 1968 Series II Land Rover. The smell of my parents' cigarettes mingled with the bulldust that seeped through every seal, vent, and open sliding window. Dad always drove, with his hands on the thin steering wheel, knuckles often white from hours of wrestling the vehicle over rocks and ruts. This was the Outback of Australia, where we would exist for months at a time before I entered my high school years. There were endless rocks and escarpments that rose from the lifeless terrain.

No air conditioning: the oppressive heat radiated through the metal frame. There was no entertainment except the stony desert, spinifex, and saltbush—and our imagination.

This is where I learned the comfort of being uncomfortable. This beautiful nothingness is where I learned everything that matters about exploration and suffering. Purposeful boredom and long-term discomfort teach you things that comfort and constant stimulation never could. That is where I learned to let my mind wander and be free. Until I was fifteen or sixteen, our family spent a significant portion of our lives away from civilization. Days driving through the Outback, with the heat so intense you could fry an egg on any metal surface. Camping in snow-capped mountains among the snow gums, where the silence was so complete it felt like pressure in your ears. Onward to a whaling station down in the Southwest of Western Australia, close to where the Southern Ocean meets the Indian Ocean.

My parents were actual explorers—not Instagram adventurers with coiffed hair and pristine make-up chasing likes and views. Dad left home at fourteen and traveled east from Perth to Melbourne. Mum, a Melbourne girl, met him through Youth Hostels Australia (YHA) while canoeing and kayaking down immense river systems on the east side of the island continent, back when there were no dams, no cell phones, no rescue, and nothing except eight to ten feet of standing waves. A car would drop them at one launch spot deep in the Snowy Mountains and pick them up seven or eight days later.

Dad has a life membership for the YHA for fighting bushfires and saving lives; Mum also has a life membership for doing the finances and helping keep those places just about financially afloat. They'd head out with hand-drawn maps on butcher's paper, a week's worth of tinned beans, salted meat, and a spectacular disregard for their own mortality.

Amazingly reckless. Beautifully naive.

This was my life.

As a kid, I'd press my face against the window until my breath fogged the glass, staring as the landscape scrolled by. Rocks older than complex life on Earth. Dirt the color of dried blood. Somewhere in those endless hours of nothing, I developed a bone-deep understanding of the idea that exploration was everything.

I recall one trip when we hadn't had real meat for over three weeks. We were surviving on tinned vegetables that tasted like the can they came in, and the occasional rabbit dad would trap—stringy, gamey things that fought back even after they were dead. We were desperate for decent animal protein.

We rolled into a remote cattle station. The homestead consisted of corrugated-iron buildings that had been bent and buckled by the Australian sun. The only meat they had left was what they fed their dogs. Scraps too tough and gristly for human consumption, they claimed. We took it anyway. We were desperate, and grateful. That night, as dusk turned to darkness, we cooked it over a fire, with the smell making our mouths water despite ourselves.

We woke up early the next morning to find the leftovers had turned green in the overnight heat.

We had eaten donkey.

That's how far off the map we were. That's how committed my parents were to the idea that exploration mattered more than comfort, and that seeing what was beyond the next ridge was worth any price. Two adults and four kids, so removed from civilization that donkey meat was just another story to tell later.

Thirty years later, I'd watch billion-dollar companies face the same kind of choice my parents made in that Land Rover. Not whether to eat spoiled meat, but whether to embrace productive discomfort or let comfort slowly spoil everything they'd built. Most chose the slow rot. They'd optimize what was working—until it stopped working. By the time they realized they needed to move, they'd forgotten how.

This book gives you the framework to choose differently. It frames business growth as a single system with two essential components, much like a tree that needs both roots and seasons.

Foundation Theory comprises the roots of your company: your Foundation, your Principles, and your Characteristics. This is WHO you are.

Explorer and Static States are your seasons. The rhythm between explosive growth and necessary consolidation—between productive discomfort and strategic rest. This is WHERE you are in the growth cycle.

Here's why both matter: A tree without roots blows over in the first storm—that's a company exploring without Foundation. A tree without seasons never grows—that's a company that is stuck optimizing yesterday forever.

Master your roots and your seasons, and you endure. Lose either, and you erode.

In business, the rot sets in long before the numbers show it. By the time your quarterly earnings start dropping and your market share had eroded, the comfortable deterioration has already been gnawing away at your Foundation for years. A team stops pushing boundaries, but their last campaign is still running strong. A company stops listening to its customers, but last year's product continues to sell. The metrics look fine. Everyone's comfortable. But the donkey meat is already starting to spoil.

The leap from the Outback to high school, and eventually into Amazon's biggest boardrooms, was never a clean arc. I was happiest trekking mountains for weeks at a time, carrying everything I needed and answering to no one but the weather. However, life doesn't reward stillness.

The determination that kept us alive in the Outback—make do, endure, and don't complain—became the same force that pushed me through international long-course triathlons, and onto the start lines at Ironman Hawaii and national championships. Different terrain. Same rules. Keep moving forward. I was world-class in terms of stubbornness.

It was hard. I lost relationships, certainty, and versions of myself that no longer fit the road ahead. However, I gained friends who became family, work that mattered, and teams bound not by comfort but by trust forged under pressure.

Each step—remote tracks, cold high country mornings, fluorescent boardrooms—taught me the same lesson: growth demands discomfort. Eat the donkey. Take on what looks impossible, one brutal, honest bite at a time, and let the foundations you were raised on carry you further than comfort ever could.

1

THE CONVERGENCE CASCADE

How optimization leads every industry toward sameness and identical mediocrity.

In the early 1990s, Russian artists Vitaly Komar and Alexander Melamid conducted an experiment. They hired a market research firm to ask 11,000 people across eleven countries what they wanted in a perfect painting. Each country got exactly what it asked for. The result should have been eleven distinct masterpieces reflecting diverse cultural preferences. Instead, each painting looked almost exactly the same.[1]

As artist Grayson Perry observed: "In nearly every country, all people really wanted was a landscape with a few figures around, animals in the foreground, mainly blue."

Komar reflected with dark humor: "Looking for freedom, we found slavery."

Flash forward to 2020, when Quibi raised $1.75 billion to revolu-

---

1. Vitaly Komar and Alexander Melamid, "The People's Choice" project, 1994-1997. Worked with polling firm Marttila & Kiley to survey approximately 11,000 people across 11 countries. Every country independently arrived at nearly identical "most wanted" paintings.

tionize mobile entertainment. They had everything: Hollywood talent, premium content, patented technology, and research showing that millennials wanted high-quality, short-form video. Eight months after launch, they shut down. They'd optimized for everything the data said people wanted—bite-sized length, portrait viewing, and commute-friendly episodes. They created exactly what their research demanded, and nobody cared. Quibi had the glitz, but missed the human context.

When you optimize for what everyone says they want, when you test your way to consensus, or when you follow best practices to their logical conclusion, you don't create something everyone loves. You make something nobody hates—and nobody remembers.

I started noticing this phenomenon in advertising agency pitches around 2018. Every deck looked identical: the same fonts (always sans serif), the same color palettes (always with that specific millennial pink or Verizon red), and the same strategic frameworks (always starting with the "consumer journey.")

We weren't copying each other. We were all independently optimizing toward the same inevitable endpoints. Like water finding the lowest point, we were all flowing toward the same creative valley. The convergence cascade is the process by which entire industries independently arrive at identical solutions through ruthless optimization. The cascade follows five predictable stages:

Stage 1: Discovery. Someone finds something that works. Edison bulbs in a coffee shop create ambiance. Sans-serif fonts test well with millennials. Grey cars hold resale value better.

Stage 2: Validation. Success breeds imitation. The coffee shop with Edison bulbs gets featured in design blogs. The brand with sans-serif fonts wins awards. The grey cars sell faster on used lots.

Stage 3: Codification. Best practices emerge. Design consultants recommend industrial fixtures. Branding agencies develop templates. Consultants tell every auto manufacturer that neutral colors optimize resale.

Stage 4: Saturation. The exception becomes the rule. Every coffee shop from Bangkok to Brooklyn has the same exposed brick and reclaimed wood. Every direct-to-consumer brand uses the same

Helvetica-inspired typeface. Eighty percent of cars are now black, white, silver, or grey—up from 40% in 1996.[2]

Stage 5: Invisibility. When everyone looks the same, no one stands out. The thing that was supposed to differentiate you becomes the thing that makes you disappear.

Elizabeth Goodspeed coined a term that describes how this happens in creative industries: the "moodboard effect."[3] Designers worldwide now draw inspiration from the same Pinterest boards, Behance galleries, and Instagram feeds. They see what works, what gets liked, and what wins awards. Without realizing it, they're all converging on the same aesthetic vocabulary.

I've lived this. Three-hour meetings debating the color of a single button in an online ad. Click-through rates would probably have been identical regardless, but no one wanted to be responsible for making the "wrong" choice. So we tested and tested until we arrived at the same blue everyone uses. Safe. Forgettable. Pointless.

If this convergence happens based on wind tunnel tests, what will happen to companies and brands from an AI perspective? Every company will look, sound, and feel exactly the same. Same pricing, same technology, same process.

Case Study: Porsche

The automotive industry exemplifies the way that technology accelerates convergence. Once manufacturers began using wind tunnels to test aerodynamics, cars began to converge on the same optimal shapes. The physics of air resistance doesn't care about brand identity. Add platform sharing—where different brands use the same underlying architecture—and the exact global safety requirements that demand specific crumple zones and sight lines, and you arrive at our current reality where the side-profile of a Hyundai Santa Fe looks like a Volvo

---

2. In fact, a 2024 study by iSeeCars showed these grayscale colors expanding from approximately 60% to 80% of market share between 2004 and 2023.
3. Godspeed described the phenomenon in AIGA's former design publication "Eye on Design" published on March 24, 2022.

XC60, looks like a Mercedes GLS. They're all within inches of each other in dimensions, and virtually identical in silhouette.

However, physics isn't destiny. Porsche proves this with the 911.

For over seventy years, the 911 has maintained its distinctive rear-engine design despite being aerodynamically "wrong." The shape creates lift at high speeds—the weight distribution challenges conventional wisdom. Every wind tunnel test indicates that it should be changed. Every engineering principle dictates moving the engine forward.

Porsche's response? They engineered around the physics rather than surrendering to it.

They developed active aerodynamics—wings that deploy at speed to counteract lift. They created sophisticated suspension systems to manage the unusual weight distribution. They turned what should be a liability into the car's defining characteristic. The 911's handling is distinctively Porsche. You can feel the engine behind you, pushing rather than pulling. It's "wrong" in a way that becomes addictively right once you drive one.

This costs more. It's harder. It requires more engineering talent, more testing, and more refinement. But it's why a 911 is instantly recognizable from a hundred yards, while most SUVs are indistinguishable at ten feet. The lesson: when everyone else surrenders to the same constraints, the company that engineers around them owns the market's only distinctive position.

Case Study: Jaguar

A brand was born in 1922 as the Swallow Sidecar, reinvented as SS Jaguar in 1935, and reforged after World War II simply as Jaguar. Their DNA (Foundation) was always clear: grace, speed, daring design, and a restless pursuit of individuality. The famous "leaper" logo wasn't decoration—it was shorthand for this Foundation. The E-Type was a sculpture at seventy miles per hour.

However, in 2024, Jaguar decided to converge. They announced that they'd phase out combustion engines, reposition themselves as an all-electric marque, and strip their visual identity down to a minimalist monogram. They traded the leaper for typography. They abandoned what they were to become what consultants said the market wanted.

The market responded with brutal clarity.[4]

Jaguar's convergence was existential. They examined Tesla's success and decided to establish themselves as another electric luxury brand. They noticed that younger buyers were favoring technology over heritage and decided to abandon their racing legacy.

Every decision was defensible. Electric is the future. Minimalism tests well with millennials. Technology matters to new buyers. However, by optimizing for what everyone else was doing, Jaguar forgot what only they could do. They traded distinctiveness for relevance and wound up with neither. The tragedy is that Jaguar could have electrified while maintaining their identity. Instead, Jaguar optimized themselves into invisibility, becoming just another luxury electric brand at precisely the moment the market was flooded with them.

The internet was supposed to democratize creativity, providing everyone with unique tools for expression. Instead, it became the world's most efficient convergence machine. With the constant rise in the use of artificial intelligence, the pace has only accelerated. Every Shopify store now uses one of the same twelve themes. Every direct-to-consumer brand follows the same playbook: pastel colors, sans-serif fonts, playful illustrations, the founder's story, a sustainability message, and Instagram-worthy packaging.

They're all responding to the same data, the same best practices, the same "proven" formulas. When everyone has access to the same infor-

---

4. Jaguar's total global annual sales dropped to 26,862 units in the 2024/2025 fiscal year (FY24/25)—an approximate 85% decline from its high of over 180,000 units in 2018 (FY17/18). This decline is calculated from Jaguar Land Rover (JLR) official financial reporting. The sales collapse was immediately visible in Europe, where new registrations in April 2025 were only 49 vehicles, marking a year-over-year sales plummet of 97.5%. This steep drop is corroborated by the European Automobile Manufacturers' Association (ACEA) data. JLR has stated that these low volumes were "in line with the company's expectations" and directly impacted by the "planned wind down of legacy Jaguar models" ahead of the launch of their new electric portfolio.

mation, makes decisions the same way, and optimizes for the same outcomes, you get convergence. The convergence cascade makes companies forget who they are. And when you forget who you are, your customers forget why they chose you.

Look at any industry, and you'll see the same pattern. Airlines are converging on the same cabin designs, loyalty programs, and fee structures. Banks offer identical apps, features, and interest rates. Streaming services with the same interfaces display the same content and employ the same recommendation algorithms. Every startup's website now looks nearly identical. They didn't hire the same designers. They use the same templates and optimize for the same metrics using the same A/B testing tools. When everyone has access to the same data, uses the same analytics platforms, and follows the same "best practices," convergence is inevitable.

Every company faces the convergence cascade—the gravitational pull toward the middle, toward safety, toward what everyone else is doing. The pressure comes from everywhere: investors want predictable returns, employees want clear direction, and customers say they want what they know. The only way out is to protect a foundational belief that no amount of data or best practices can replace.

2

WELCOME TO AVERAGE

Why being average ensures slow extinction, and why AI is making a world where average is "good enough."

In August 2025, Chip Cutter wrote a piece in the Wall Street Journal called: "AI Is Coming for the Consultants. Inside McKinsey, 'This Is Existential.'"

McKinsey. The firm that turns Ivy League graduates into millionaires. The invisible hand behind most Fortune 500 decisions. The gold standard of strategic thinking. They'd just cut their workforce by 5,000 while simultaneously rolling out 12,000 AI agents.

Kate Smaje, the senior partner leading McKinsey's AI efforts, revealed the new reality with brutal honesty: "Traditionally, a strategy project with a client might require an engagement manager plus 14 consultants. Today, it might need an engagement manager plus two or three consultants, alongside a few AI agents."

The frameworks McKinsey charges millions to apply? An AI can be trained on their decades of confidential reports and generate solutions that apply that past knowledge (acquired by humans) toward new projects. The market analysis that took teams of consultants weeks to compile is done in minutes. The competitive benchmarking that justified their fees can be automated and available to anyone with a laptop. On the one hand, McKinsey, Bain, BCG, and the rest are all accelerating the convergence cascade in their own right. They aren't malicious; their methodology naturally pushes companies toward the same answers. On the other hand, the rise of AI has codified these best practices and democratized them, thereby exponentially multiplying the average.

Here's the real rub: if all the consultancies are doing the same thing, with basically the same information, and advising a similar set of clients, then what is going to make your company and brand stand out in the years to come? When McKinsey advises every CPG company to "focus on millennial consumers," when Bain tells every retailer to "invest in omnichannel," and when BCG advises every manufacturer to "digitize supply chain," entire industries begin to move in lockstep. The consultants just do what they're paid to do: reduce risk through proven solutions. However, proven solutions are, by definition, solutions that already exist. You can't optimize your way to differentiation.

McKinsey's own research becomes its epitaph: they studied company lifespans on the S&P 500 and found the average tenure dropped from 61 years in 1958 to just 18 years by 2012. It's projected to shrink to 12 years by 2027.[1] These weren't companies that failed spectacularly. They were companies that performed adequately until being adequate was no longer enough.

If the arbiters of business excellence can be replaced by code, what does that say about the excellence they were arbitrating? When the best strategic thinking can be automated, "above average" becomes meaningless. Now that everyone has access to the best practices and formulas recommended by experts, average is now the ceiling.

The insidious aspect of the average is how we've normalized it through metrics that make mediocrity look like success. We use spreadsheets to lie to ourselves. We celebrate adequacy because a number on a dashboard permits us to be mediocre. I'm going to show you how metrics like NPS and engagement scores are masking a slow

---

1. McKinsey & Company, *Six building blocks for creating a high-performing digital enterprise*, McKinsey Digital, 2015. The report cites Standard & Poor's data showing S&P 500 company lifespans declining from 61 years in 1958 to 18 years in 2011, with projections that 75% of current incumbents will vanish by 2027.

leak in the hull of your business—and how companies like Southwest deliberately choose strategic "terribleness" over being average.

A Net Promoter Score (NPS) measures whether customers would recommend you. Most companies celebrate anything above zero— literally just breaking even between promoters and detractors. The average NPS across all industries hovers around 30. For every three people who love you enough to recommend you, two are indifferent, and one actively discourages others.

You're bleeding customers so slowly you don't notice it until you're already underwater. Companies treat 30 as "good enough" because everyone else is also at 30. It's the hubris of benchmarking against mediocrity rather than asking what "great" actually looks like.

Gallup's research shows that only around 33% of employees are engaged at work.[2] Companies treat it as usual, acceptable, and even reasonable if they're slightly above average. Think about what we're accepting: two-thirds of our workforce is either going through the motions or actively undermining our success. We've normalized organizational mediocrity.

This acceptance of average engagement eventually creates a death spiral:

1. Engaged employees carry the load for everyone
2. They burn out from the unfair burden
3. They either disengage or leave
4. The percentage of disengaged employees grows
5. Company performance declines
6. The company responds with cost cuts and "efficiency"
7. The remaining engaged employees further disengage

Byron Sharp's *How Brands Grow* revealed that average brands require above-average spending to maintain their position. When you have nothing distinctive to say, you have to say it louder and more often, even to be noticed.

---

2. Only 23% of employees worldwide and just 33% in the U.S. were engaged according to Gallup's 2021 State of the Global Workplace report.

Case Study: Southwest Airlines

Southwest Airlines was profitable for 47 consecutive years—from 1973 through 2019—surviving recessions, terrorist attacks, and fuel crises while American, United, and Delta cycled through bankruptcies. The pandemic broke the streak briefly in 2020-2021, but Southwest returned to profitability while maintaining its foundation. During its peak years, Southwest's operating margins were consistently twice the industry average.[3]

Southwest figured out something most airlines miss: you can't be great at everything. They're deliberately terrible at everything other airlines consider essential.

No assigned seats. No first class. No meals. No hub-and-spoke system. No international routes for decades. By traditional airline metrics, they're below average at almost everything. However, Southwest understood that you can't be great at everything. More importantly, you shouldn't even try.

What Southwest chose to be extraordinary at is getting you from Point A to Point B cheaply, and on time, with a smile. That's it.

Every "terrible" choice makes them better at their one thing. No assigned seats means faster boarding. No first class means more passengers. No meals means faster turnarounds. No hubs means no cascade delays.

Herb Kelleher, Southwest's legendary CEO, had a simple framework: "Will this help us be a low-cost airline?" If yes, do it. If no, don't. If uncertain, the answer is no.

This clarity requires saying no to profitable opportunities, no to customer requests, and no to industry standards. It requires you to be comfortable with people choosing your competitors. The average airline tries to serve everyone. Southwest serves exactly one customer: someone who values low cost and reliability. Everyone else can fly elsewhere.

---

3. Southwest Airlines reported its 47th consecutive year of profitability in January 2019 (Southwest Airlines investor relations). In 2019, Southwest's operating margin was 13.2% compared to the transportation industry median of 8.1% (IBA Group, February 2025).

Their employees don't apologize for what Southwest doesn't offer. They celebrate what it does. Flight attendants rap safety instructions. Pilots crack jokes. Gate agents run boarding games. They've turned constraints into character. The customers who choose Southwest love them precisely because they're not average. They become evangelists because Southwest solves their specific problem better than anyone else. They forgive the weaknesses because the strength is so clear.

Case Study: Cracker Barrel

In August 2025, Cracker Barrel updated its logo and modernized their appearance. The stock shed almost $100 million in market value that week, plunging more than 12%[4]—all because of a logo.

Except it wasn't just about the logo. It was about what happens when you optimize the wrong thing. At its foundation, Cracker Barrel wasn't in the business of modern casual dining. They were selling nostalgia—your grandmother's kitchen in restaurant form. A place where time moved more slowly, where biscuits came in baskets, and where the gift shop sold candy you hadn't seen since childhood.[5] Their customers were purchasing a feeling.

"The way we communicate, the things on the menu, the way the stores look and feel... All of these things came up time and time again in our research as opportunities for us to really regain relevancy," said CEO Julie Felss Masino .[6] She assumed the problem was the packaging, rather than understanding what customers actually valued.

There's that word. Relevancy. Code for modern. Code for what everyone else is doing. Code for average.

Cracker Barrel's customers chose them precisely because they weren't modern. While the industry rushed toward fast-casual

---

4. CNN Business, "Cracker Barrel stock tanks after unveiling a controversial logo change," August 21, 2025.

5. The chances are the candy had also been there since your childhood.

6. This quote came from CEO Julie Felss Masino's May 2024 presentation to analysts, where she laid out the company's diagnosis and remedies for their relevancy issues. CNN Business reported on it in June 2024, several months before the actual logo change in August 2025.

concepts, ghost kitchens, and QR code menus, Cracker Barrel was defiantly analog. That wasn't a bug. It was the entire feature. When they updated the logo—making it cleaner, text-only, and more contemporary—they signaled something devastating: we're embarrassed by what we are.

The customer response was swift and brutal. Social media users called the new logo "soulless," "bland," and "generic." One wrote that "changing the logo just feels like another little piece of culture dying off."

Within weeks, Cracker Barrel reverted to their original design. However, the damage was done. They'd confused their Foundation (nostalgia and unchanging comfort) for a disposable Characteristic (the visual identity). They'd looked at their distinctiveness and decided average looked safer.

Was it the brand agency's fault? No. The agency didn't wake up one morning and decide to erase Uncle Herschel. Someone at Cracker Barrel briefed them to modernize. Someone approved the direction. Someone said yes to the final design. When the backlash hit, leadership blamed the consultants rather than owning their decision.

They'd outsourced the hardest questions: What makes us distinctive? What do we refuse to change? What productive discomfort are we avoiding by chasing "relevancy"?

Southwest chose strategic terribleness and stayed profitable for 47 years. Cracker Barrel optimized toward relevancy and lost $100 million in a week. The difference wasn't in their agencies. It was in their willingness to eat the donkey.

The gravitational pull toward average is powerful because it feels safe. No one gets fired for average performance. No one gets sued for average products. No one gets criticized for average decisions.

McKinsey's transformation from fifteen consultants on a project to three humans and some code isn't just their problem—it's a preview of every industry's future. When strategic thinking can be automated, when optimization can be achieved by anyone with a laptop, and when best practices spread instantly, average becomes obsolete. Gap, Sears, and Borders achieved perfect averageness and became invisible. Southwest chose strategic terribleness and has been profitable for nearly five decades.

Average is not a sustainable position. It's not a Foundation on which you can build. It's not a safe harbor to rest in. Average is where companies go to vanish into irrelevance, surrounded by other average companies, all wondering why customers can't tell them apart. You can aim for something acceptable and achieve something invisible. If you try to please everyone, it will ultimately matter to no one. You can benchmark yourself to death. Or you can choose what to be terrible at, accept that some people will hate you, and build something that matters to the people who matter to you.

3
FOUNDATIONS

The unchanging core that lets you transform without losing yourself.

If you don't know who you are, the market will tell you who to be, and that path leads to average. We've covered the danger of convergence. Now we pivot to the antidote: Foundation Theory (visualized by the pyramid of Foundations as the bottom layer, Principles as the middle layer, and Characteristics as the top layer). This is the non-negotiable architecture of your company, the core that never changes, and it's built in the messy, uncomfortable, early days. I'm going to show you what your Foundation looks like, and why you must define it before you try to change anything else.

When I interviewed for a senior role at Kohler, they included something I'd never encountered during an executive interview. Senior positions typically include personality trait assessments, but this was a psychological evaluation designed to understand my Foundations—the experiences and conditions that shaped who I became before I even knew who I wanted to be. The assessment sought to identify patterns in my invisible architecture. How did I respond to authority? What drove my risk tolerance? Where did my confidence come from, and what eroded it? This was the bedrock beneath my professional persona, built during the formative years when my brain was still wiring itself.

One question kept surfacing as I worked through the assessment: "Describe a time when you had to adapt to circumstances beyond your control." My mind went immediately to that Land Rover, to the Outback, to the moment we realized we'd eaten spoiled donkey meat. That experience taught me that discomfort isn't failure, that adaptation matters more than comfort, and that you can survive what seems impossible if you're willing to face it.

That's what foundational years do. They give you frameworks for interpreting everything that comes after.

Growing up in advertising reinforced this lesson. The period of my career when I won most awards came during what I call my season of discontent—living half in New Zealand, half in Australia, working phenomenally long hours for agencies that billed for every second we spent on their clients' work. The hours were brutal. The pressure was relentless.

However, the rewards made it worthwhile. We had freedom to experiment with budgets, timelines, and creative approaches, because the trust was there. The agency made money off our time, so they let us use that time however we needed. We made mistakes. We learned from them. We built campaigns that won awards, because we were given room to fail without fear of immediate consequences.

It was about adaptation. When you're working that hard, you either learn to adjust to circumstances beyond your control or you burn out. I learned to adjust.

Psychologists call these "formative years" for a reason. Erik Erikson mapped them as stages—trust vs. mistrust, autonomy vs. shame, initiative vs. guilt—each one building on the last like layers of sediment.[1] If trust doesn't form in the first layer, everything above it tilts.

---

1. Erik Erikson, developmental psychologist and psychoanalyst, proposed eight stages of psychosocial development spanning the entire lifespan. The first three stages—trust vs. mistrust (infancy), autonomy vs. shame and doubt (toddlerhood), and initiative vs. guilt (preschool age)—establish the psychological foundation upon which later development is built. Erikson, E. H. (1968). *Identity: Youth and Crisis*. New York: W. W. Norton & Company.

Carol Dweck proved it works cognitively too: children who learn that persistence leads to success develop different neural patterns to those who believe that effort is futile.[2] Those patterns become the operating system for adult decisions.

You can renovate a building, but you can't ignore its foundations. Add floors, change the facade, reimagine the interior—if the foundations crack, everything fails.

My Foundation was built on dust, curiosity, and productive discomfort. The Outback taught me to make the most of what I had. That became my framework for leadership: don't wait for perfect conditions; instead, make progress with what's available. The foundation wasn't glamorous, but it proved unshakeable.

Every organization or department has the same formative period—those early, scrappy stages when a few people, usually under-resourced and overcommitted, decide to build something that doesn't yet exist. That's when a company's real DNA forms: in the decisions, tensions, and trade-offs that define its early survival.

Think of Amazon's foundational years, when Jeff Bezos used an office door as a desk. The obsession with customers was an existential necessity. Without fanatical customer loyalty, there would be no second chance. Every decision—from pricing and packaging to customer service response times—was filtered through one question: "What does the customer need?" That question, asked and answered thousands of times during those early years, became the foundation of Amazon.

Years ago, I spoke with one of Amazon's early leaders, delving into what the company actually stands for. His answer was simple—four lines that Bezos would repeat like mantras: "It's always Day 1." "Start with the customer and work backwards." "We're willing to be misunderstood for long periods of time." "Good intentions don't work. Mechanisms do."

Stay uncomfortable. Focus relentlessly on who you are serving. Build systems that keep you in motion. That's the Foundation. When

---

2. Carol S. Dweck, *Mindset: The New Psychology of Success* (New York: Random House, 2006)

the company scaled to millions of employees, those beliefs remained constant even as everything else evolved.

Apple's foundational years were about the belief that design and emotion could be inseparable. When Steve Jobs and Steve Wozniak started in that garage, they were creating something entirely new. They were proving that technology could be beautiful, that products could feel human, and that the intersection of liberal arts and engineering could create something transcendent. That Foundation, formed during years of struggle and rejection, became the unchanging truth that guided every product decision for the next forty years.

Airbnb's Foundation wasn't hospitality—it was belonging. When Brian Chesky and Joe Gebbia couldn't afford their rent in San Francisco, they decided to rent out air mattresses in their apartment to conference attendees, discovering something more than a business model in the process. They found that people craved authentic connection with places and communities. Their Foundation, "belonging anywhere," was formed during those desperate early months when survival meant understanding what guests actually needed, not what the hospitality industry thought they wanted.

Each of these companies faced "donkey moments"—uncomfortable, messy, improvised survival phases that forged their identity. Amazon shipped books from a garage with no climate control. Apple was rejected by investors who couldn't see the value in making computers beautiful. Airbnb's founders survived on cereal they called "Obama O's" and "Cap'n McCain's" to fund the business. These were the experiences that created the foundations those companies would stand on forever.

When a company scales, it starts to layer process, structure, and hierarchy on top of its Foundation. This is necessary—you can't run a billion-dollar company the way you run a garage startup. But slowly, the foundational instincts fade into the background. You hire specialists who weren't there when the donkey was eaten, and suddenly, decisions are being made by people who don't know what hunger feels like. The company begins to wobble.

Your Foundations are your company's anchor. You can swing at the mooring and still be safe—the wind shifts, the current changes, and storms roll through, but the anchor holds you in place. You know where you are. You can adjust your position, but you're tethered to something solid. Break that anchor line, and you drift. Not knowing where you're going. Not even knowing you're moving, until you look up and realize you're miles from where you started, heading toward rocks you never saw coming.

Jim Collins studied this pattern extensively in *How the Mighty Fall*. He found that the first stage of failure in great companies isn't financial loss—it's hubris born of success. A belief that what worked before will work forever. Companies forget the discomfort that forged their resilience. They drift from their foundational truths, replacing conviction with comfort. They cut the anchor line without realizing it, thinking they're free when, in fact, they're just lost.

From 2003 to 2008, I worked at an advertising agency whose biggest client was Washington Mutual Bank. Generally, it was a dream account: a major financial institution with a clear purpose, a fun brand, and, more importantly, good marketing clients. We worked on a lot of their business. Branding, credit cards, free checking, store design, and home loans. All was good. Except something felt wrong from the moment I walked onto the home loan floors in their Seattle head-quarters.

Suddenly, the friendly WaMu was no longer a bank. It was a boiler room. Home loan experts were hard-sell salespeople targeting subprime customers—working phones like traders, chasing commissions, and pushing mortgages with the energy of a used-car lot on the last day of the month. These weren't bankers helping families find homes; they were sharks. The irony was that WaMu had been founded in 1889, right after the Great Seattle Fire, specifically to help working people rebuild their homes and their lives. The Foundation was literally about stability and trust—assisting ordinary citizens in recovering from disasters and building something lasting. For over a century, that's precisely what they had done. They were the boring bank, the reliable bank, the bank that helped immigrants and factory workers buy their first homes.

However, somewhere in the race for growth, that Foundation had been replaced. "Helping Americans own homes" morphed into "selling as many mortgages as possible." The metrics shifted from customer stability to loan volume. The incentives changed from long-term relationships to short-term transactions—selling subprime loans to people with thin or poor FICO scores. When I'd present strategic business and marketing concepts, the feedback was always the same: "Make it sell harder." Not "Does this build trust?" or "Does this help our customers?" Just "Will this move more products?" They abandoned banking and became a sales machine.

In September 2008, Washington Mutual collapsed—the largest bank failure in U.S. history. Everyone blamed the financial crisis, the subprime mortgage meltdown, and the broader economic conditions. However, unknowingly, I'd watched the real failure happen years earlier, in those conference rooms where quarterly targets mattered more than foundational purpose.

The failure was a slow drift. WaMu stopped asking, "How do we help people build stable lives?" and started asking, "How do we sell more mortgages?" They confused their mechanism (mortgages) with their meaning (stability). When you lose your Foundation, you fail spectacularly. In this case, they brought millions of innocent people down with them.

Legacy brands, in particular, fall into this trap. They hire consultants to rediscover their "why," when the "why" was never lost—it was simply buried under layers of process and pride. The best ideas usually come from the people closest to the work. The craftspeople who still pour things by hand. The designers who still sketch rather than default to software. The marketers who still believe the brand can be bold. These people haven't forgotten the Foundation. They're still in touch with what makes the company matter. They haven't been promoted far enough away from the work to lose sight of it.

Many companies do this backwards. They promote individuals who understand the Foundation, then assign them jobs that have nothing to do with it. The factory worker who knows the craft becomes a manager who reviews spreadsheets. The designer who understands quality becomes a director who attends meetings about the process. The marketer who has conviction becomes a VP who optimizes for consensus. Then the board wonders why nobody remembers what the company stands for.

The first stage of decline is forgetting. Companies forget the discomfort that forged their resilience. They drift from their foundational truths, replacing conviction with comfort. The challenging aspect of Foundations is that you can't see them until you need them. When everything's going well, who cares what you're built on? However, when the market shifts, when competitors emerge, or when customers change—that's when you find out if your Foundation can hold weight or if you've been building on sand the whole time.

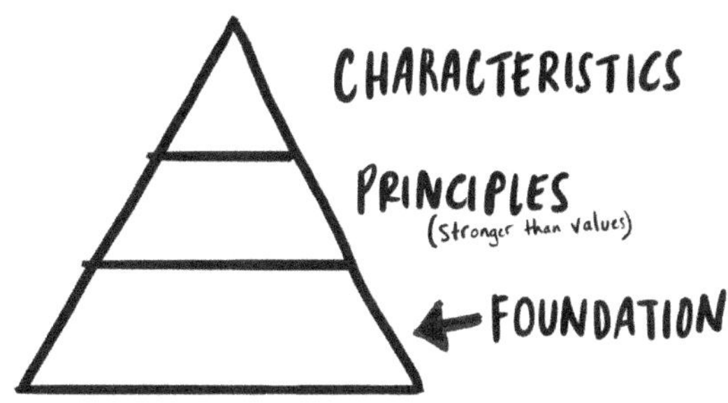

When you ask an executive, "What business are you in?" you can usually tell within ten seconds whether the company has a strong Foundation or not.

Weak answers focus on products, categories, or markets:

- "We're in the bathroom fixtures business"
- "We're a coffee company"
- "We're in cloud computing"

These answers are incomplete. They describe the output, not the input. They define what you sell, not who or what you stand for. Strong answers articulate purpose:

- Howard Schultz: "Starbucks isn't in the coffee business serving people, we're in the people business serving coffee"
- Nike: "Our mission is to bring inspiration and innovation to every athlete in the world"
- Amazon: "We're in the business of removing friction between people and what they want"

These are Foundations made visible through language. When Schultz says Starbucks is in the people business, he's articulating the foundational truth that guides every decision—from store design to employee benefits to why they write your name on cups. The coffee serves as a vessel for human connection (the Foundation).

When Nike says they serve athletes, they're not defining "athlete" narrowly. Their Foundation is democratizing human potential through movement—everyone who has a body is an athlete. That Foundation, formed during Phil Knight's early days selling shoes from his car trunk, shapes everything from their advertising and their product design to their stance on social issues.

When Amazon says they remove friction, they're articulating the foundational obsession that drove every innovation—from one-click ordering to pre-populating past customer information in the 1990s to Prime and AWS. Jeff Bezos cared about making it easier for people to get what they needed. That Foundation guided decisions that seemed insane at the time but proved prescient in retrospect.

Most companies confuse what they sell with what they stand for. The category is just the vessel—the Foundation lies beneath. Airbnb is in the belonging business. Apple is in the human potential business. Amazon is in the convenience business. Kohler is in the gracious living business.

Case Study: Michelin

In 1900, André and Édouard Michelin faced an existential problem. There were approximately 3,000 cars in all of France. Their tire factory could produce 200 tires per day—enough to replace every tire in the country in a couple of months.

Any consultant would have told them to scale down. Any MBA would have shown them the TAM (Total Addressable Market) and recommended that they find a different business. The obvious move was to optimize for the existing market.

Instead, the Michelin brothers asked themselves: what business are we actually in?

Movement was the answer. And movement without a destination is meaningless.

So they published a restaurant guide. Not a tire catalog. Not maintenance tips. A guide to restaurants and hotels worth driving to— places in towns most French people had never heard of, destinations you couldn't reach by train, spots that required you to own one of those 3,000 cars.

The Michelin brothers knew their Foundation.

They were in the mobility business, and mobility needs a reason to exist. People buy tires because tires take them somewhere worth going. Publishing restaurant guides seems less random once you understand this. You're not advertising tires; you're creating reasons for tires to exist.

By 1914, France had over 100,000 cars. By 1920, France had over 230,000 cars.[3] The Michelin Guide had become so essential that Michelin started charging for it—and people paid. By 1926, they had begun awarding stars to exceptional restaurants, creating a rating system so powerful that chefs would later commit suicide when they lost one.

---

3. France had 233,065 vehicles in circulation in 1920, up from 107,535 in 1914. Historical data from Comité des Constructeurs Français d'Automobiles (CCFA), the French automotive industry trade association, as cited in Best Selling Cars Blog, January 2019.

A tire company had become the world's most influential arbiter of culinary excellence.

What you manufacture is just the delivery mechanism. Get that wrong, and no amount of optimization or innovation will save you. Get it right, and you can create markets that don't yet exist.

Case Study: Kohler

Cast iron is more than nostalgia to Kohler. Cast iron is literally what Kohler is made of—it's heavy, it requires genuine craftsmanship to shape, and you can't fake it. It either holds water or it doesn't. That's what a Foundation is—the thing that can't be faked, can't be optimized away, and can't be pivoted from when the market shifts. It's what you're made of, not what you make.

Kohler is a 152+-year-old company that makes kitchen and bath products. That's what sits in the warehouse. But that's not their Foundation. John Michael Kohler built housing for European immigrants coming to Wisconsin toward the end of World War I.

He helped them get American citizenship. Graciousness was a part of the Foundation from the beginning. Kohler thinks about kitchens as gathering spaces and bathrooms as transformation spaces. When you're stressed from work, you can take a long, hot shower or have a soak. When you're celebrating a milestone, the kitchen is where people end up. The products enable those moments—they don't create them. Kohler is in the business of transforming spaces with graciousness, they just happen to use plumbing products to do it.

Should Kohler make cheaper faucets to compete on price? No—that would cheapen the transformation. Should they focus only on wealthy customers? No—everyone deserves spaces that transform them. The products change. The markets shift. But the Foundation—graciousness and transformation—that doesn't move.

The Principles guide how Kohler lives that Foundation: One single level of quality. This operates as a filter. Before launching anything, they ask: "If we do this, are we giving customers the best experience possible?" If the answer is no, the Foundation holds steady while the Principle just stopped you from making a bad decision.

When you plan Foundation-first, you avoid the slow drift. You don't wake up five years later, wondering how you got into businesses that have nothing to do with who you are. When your Foundation drives planning, saying "no" becomes easier. You have clarity. You're asking: does this strengthen or dilute the Foundation?

When Michelin published a restaurant guide instead of scaling down production, it looked radical. When Amazon kept reinvesting every dollar back into infrastructure and customer experience instead of taking profits, Wall Street thought Bezos was reckless. However, each decision makes sense once you understand their Foundations. If you're in the mobility business, restaurant guides are obvious. If you're in the transformation business, fake people undermine everything. If you're in the obsessive customer service business, anything that measurably improves the customer experience is worth the investment—even if it delays profitability.

Amazon wasn't throwing money at failures. Customer satisfaction was rising. Selection was expanding. Delivery times were shrinking. They just weren't optimizing for quarterly earnings—they were optimizing for their Foundation. There's a critical difference: they invested where they saw impact aligned with customer obsession, and they killed initiatives that didn't serve customers, regardless of sunk costs.

Michelin still manufactures tires. They've also expanded into shipping container seals, maps, digital navigation, and hotel guides. The products changed. The Foundation didn't.

Amazon started with books, added everything else, and then launched cloud computing services. Completely different products. Same Foundation: remove friction from customers' lives.

Apple went from computers to phones to watches to services. Different products. Same Foundation: technology should feel human.

If your Foundation only makes sense with your current product, you don't have a Foundation. You have a product strategy wearing a disguise.

Your Foundation isn't your mission statement. Those are usually meaningless—committee wordsmithing corporate speak until every edge is sanded off. Your Foundation isn't your values. Every company claims to value "integrity" and "innovation." Table stakes, not differentiators. Your Foundation isn't your origin story. Nike started selling shoes out of a car trunk. That's a great story, but it's not their Foundation. Their Foundation enables human potential through movement—the car trunk was just where they began.

Brands change. Foundations don't.

Your Foundation is the unchanging truth that lets you transform without losing yourself. It's heavier than strategy, deeper than culture, and more durable than any product you'll ever make. Defining what business you're genuinely in forces you to strip back everything that has drifted—the slogans, the quarterly goals, and the organizational charts—and return to the core truth that gives meaning to all of it. That definition becomes your grounding, your "why." Everything that follows—your Principles, your Characteristics, and your brand expression—is built on top of it. Most companies have no idea what theirs is until it's too late to make a difference.

4
PRINCIPLES

How do you make decisions when no one's watching?

Your Foundation tells you who you are, but your Principles show up when it matters most—when the decision is expensive, unpopular, or requires sacrificing short-term profit for long-term conviction.

My coaches used to say, "It's what you do when no one is watching that makes a difference." Principles work the same way. Do you pick up the dog poop when nobody's around to see you do it? That's the test—not whether you have values printed on the wall, but whether you follow them when there's no audience, no reward, and no recognition. Principles are fixed rules of engagement that flow directly from your Foundation. I'm going to show you the difference between an aspirational value statement and a real Principle—and why the real ones usually come with a price tag.

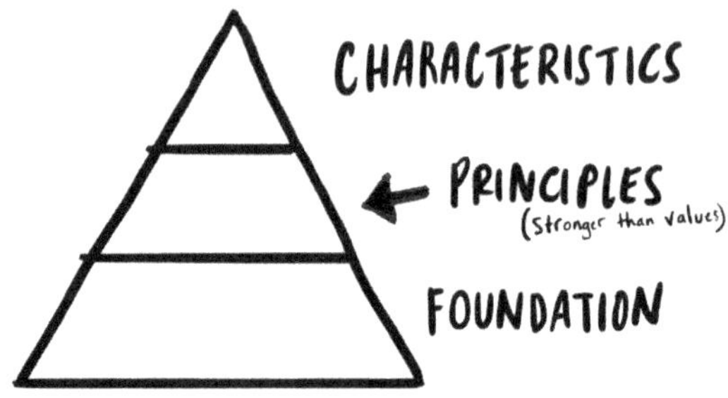

In 2022, when Russia invaded Ukraine, Airbnb could have issued a statement. They could have donated. They could have done what most companies do: acknowledge the tragedy and move on. Instead, within days of the invasion, CEO Brian Chesky committed to housing 100,000 Ukrainian refugees for free. Airbnb and its founders contributed $17 million, with over 21,500 hosts signing up to help—including 14,000 who weren't even existing Airbnb hosts. California wildfires, Hurricane Sandy in 2012—same response. Since Airbnb.org's founding, more than 1.6 million nights of free housing have been provided to over 250,000 people across multiple countries. When the LA fires hit in January 2025, 6,500 people gained access to emergency housing within two days.[1]

Airbnb's Foundation is belonging. They're in the business of creating spaces where everyone feels welcome. That's what they do. But their Principle is how they do it when it costs them: when people have nowhere to go, how fast can we house them? Not "let's have a meeting about this." Not "what's the ROI?" Just "how fast?"

Your Foundation tells you what business you're in. Your Principles guide how you operate within that Foundation, especially when it's expensive. Chesky calls this a "principle decision"—you don't know how it's going to end, so you ask how you want to be remembered regardless of the outcome. The decision wasn't universally popular.

---

1. Statistics from Airbnb.org impact reports and press releases, 2022-2025.

Housing refugees doesn't show up as revenue growth. But Chesky moved forward anyway.

The Principle wasn't negotiable. Compare that to companies with beautiful statements. "We put customers first." "We value innovation." "We believe in community." Then a crisis hits, and suddenly there are budget constraints, competing priorities, and stakeholder concerns.

Airbnb's Principle cost them $17 million for Ukraine alone, and tens of millions more over thirteen years. It involved executive time coordinating nonprofits instead of optimizing conversions, and customer service infrastructure diverted from paying customers to people in crisis. When customers see you sacrifice profits to stay true to Principles, they stop comparing your prices to competitors. They're no longer buying a transaction. At least in some part, they're buying what you stand for.

Case Study: CVS

In 2014, CVS discontinued cigarette sales. They walked away from $2 billion in annual revenue—17% of their front-of-store sales. Wall Street analysts called it financial suicide. Competitors kept selling cigarettes. However, CVS had a Principle problem. They'd positioned themselves as a healthcare company. "Helping people on their path to better health" was their stated purpose. Selling cigarettes while claiming to care about health was hypocrisy.

Cigarettes weren't always a problem. When CVS was primarily a convenience store that filled prescriptions, selling cigarettes made sense. But as they added MinuteClinics, expanded pharmacy services, and targeted chronic disease management, the Principle of "health first" conflicted with cartons of Marlboros behind the counter. They could have ignored the contradiction. They could have told themselves that cigarette customers and pharmacy customers were different people (they weren't). Instead, they acknowledged that their Principle had evolved and their products needed to catch up. This is what Principle-driven decision-making looks like. It's expensive, and it hurts.[2]

---

2. CVS acquired MinuteClinic in 2006. MinuteClinic expanded from treating seven

Front-store sales dropped 8% after tobacco was removed. The Principle cost them revenue they never recovered. There was no fairy-tale ending where health systems rewarded them with new business—CVS's pharmacy growth came from acquiring Caremark in 2007, giving them control over prescription benefit management for 80% of the market. That had nothing to do with the tobacco decision. The Principle was expensive, and it stayed expensive. However, it removed the hypocrisy in the clash between what they claimed to stand for and what they actually sold.

Case Study: Patagonia

Patagonia started as a climbing equipment company. Yvon Chouinard, the founder, was a climber himself. He made pitons—metal spikes you hammer into rock to secure your rope. They were reusable and durable: the best in the business. Climbers loved them. But Chouinard noticed something: the rock faces at popular climbing spots were getting destroyed. Every piton placement scarred the rock. Multiply that by thousands of climbers, and Yosemite's granite was turning into Swiss cheese.

He faced a choice: continue making the product that built his business, or evolve his Principles about what his company stands for. In 1972, he stopped making pitons entirely and switched to aluminum chocks that didn't damage rock. This was not a minor adjustment. Pitons were their core product. The margin was good. Climbers weren't demanding alternatives—most didn't even realize they were causing damage. However, Chouinard had a Principle: leave the mountain better than you found it. Once he saw the contradiction, he couldn't unsee it.

The Principle remained—protect the places we love—but how it was expressed evolved. From pitons to chocks. Later, from pure climbing gear to clothing made with environmental principles. Then, to advocating for the protection of public lands. Each evolution made

---

acute illnesses to offering over 65 services including chronic disease management. CVS removed all tobacco products from its stores in 2014.

sense because the Principle was clear. This is different from flip-flopping. Flip-flopping is changing your Principles to follow profit. Evolution is changing your methods as you understand the Principles better. Can you trace a straight line from your original Principle to your current one? With Patagonia, you can. In 1972, it was "Don't destroy the mountains"—this became "Don't destroy the planet" by the 2020s. Same Principle, broader application.

In 2010, I was in Birmingham, Alabama, after a client presentation. It was brutally hot, over 100 degrees. Our team found a traditional Southern gentleman's restaurant—jackets required. After the meeting, one of my colleagues, Michael, rolled up his sleeves. He had a tattoo of Stevie Wonder on his arm.

Shortly after, we were politely asked to leave.

The message was clear. At the time, I assumed it was their policy against tattoos—some old-fashioned rule about ink being unprofessional.

We learned later that they had been objecting to a tattoo of a black man on a white man's arm.

This was 2010.

It was one of the most uncomfortable moments of my life—realizing we had been escorted from an establishment because my colleague honored a black artist on his own body. We were being judged for an image of skin on skin.

That bar had a Principle. A racist Principle, but a Principle nonetheless. They were willing to lose paying customers—well-dressed professionals on corporate expense accounts—to enforce it.

Principles cost something regardless of whether they're noble or reprehensible. That bar owner sacrificed revenue for his beliefs. CVS sacrificed $2 billion for theirs. The difference is what you're paying for.

However, there's a danger here worth noting. Principles can become prisons.

Kodak had a Principle: capture moments on film. That Principle built an empire. However, with the advent of digital photography, they treated the Principle as an unchanging Foundation. They couldn't evolve from "film" to "capturing moments," because they'd confused the method with the purpose. This is an art, knowing when to defend your Principles and when to evolve them. The Foundation doesn't change, but the Principles need to breathe.

Ask: does this Principle help us fulfill our Foundation, or has it become an obstacle to it? If Patagonia's Principle were "make pitons forever," it would have become an obstacle to their Foundation of protecting mountains. When they shifted to chocks, the Principle evolved, but the Foundation held.

Don't confuse your Foundation with Principle, or else you'll treat everything as sacred, then wonder why you're inflexible. Or else you'll treat everything as negotiable, and then wonder why you have no identity. Foundations are forever. Principles can evolve, if you are careful about how you do it. Some companies write their Principles in corporate speak, and then wonder why no one follows them. For instance: "We empower stakeholders through synergistic collaboration." What does that even mean?

"Customer-centricity" is jargon. It's abstract. Nobody actually says, "We should be more customer-centric here" in a real meeting. They say, "We're ignoring what customers actually want." Amazon's "customer obsession" works because the language is concrete enough to use in real conversations. You'll hear, "I'm not sure that's customer-obsessed" as an actual argument against a decision. The Principle is simple enough to deploy in real-time, specific enough to mean something, and memorable enough that people actually say it aloud. It is jargon, as opposed to plain language. In general, I have found that real Principles should be able to pass three tests:

1. The Conversation Test: Do people actually use these words in meetings? If your Principle is "stakeholder alignment" but no one says that phrase aloud, it's not a real Principle. It's a decoration.

2. The Trade-off Test: Has this Principle ever cost you something? If your Principle is "quality" but you've never actually sacrificed speed or cost for quality, it's not a Principle—it's an aspiration. A Principle should be divisive, and not be open to any grey areas.

3. The Evolution Test: Can you trace how this Principle has evolved, and does each evolution make sense given what you have learned?

If your Principles change every time you get a new CEO, they're not Principles—they're whatever that leader felt like writing. Real Principles outlast individual leaders because they're rooted in the Foundation. CVS walked away from $2 billion. Patagonia has spent millions advocating for environmental policies that make their business harder. Principles cost money. That's how you know they're real.

The companies that fail here are the ones that write Principles they have no intention of following. They put "integrity" on the wall while cooking the books. They claim "people first" while stack-ranking employees and firing the bottom 10%. The Principles become cynicism generators—visible proof that leadership doesn't mean what they say. This is worse than having no Principles at all. At least without Principles, people can't point to hypocrisy. However, when you say. "We value work-life balance" and then expect people to work 70-hour weeks, you've created a weapon that employees will use against you.

Principles don't need to be noble. Southwest's Principle: fast turn-arounds through operational simplicity—isn't humanitarian. It's ruthlessly commercial. However, it costs them in terms of opportunities to pursue other business. Amazon's customer obsession means they'll lose money acquiring customers if it builds long-term trust. What matters is whether following the Principle costs you something—and whether it connects directly to your Foundation. Watch how the working Principles actually function.

Meetings: Someone proposes a decision. You test it against your Principles. "Does this align with [Principle]?" Yes? Move forward. No? Stop. Unclear? Your Principle needs work.

Hiring: Most companies hire for skills and hope for cultural fit. Reverse this. Filter by Principles first. If your Principle is excellence, you hire top talent who want to work with other top talent. Someone who values job security over excellence is filtered out before you look at their resume.

Conflict: Two people disagree. Usually, they're optimizing for different Principles without realizing it. Make the Principles explicit.

The conflict often disappears when everyone sees they are serving the same purpose.

Reviews: Most performance reviews ask what you accomplished. A better question is: what Principles did you embody? At Amazon, you are evaluated on leadership Principles. Did you show customer obsession? Did you show a bias for action? The behaviors matter more than the outcomes. Principles consistently applied create sustainable results.

This is the difference between working Principles and wall art. They're not decorative. They're functional. They're the operating system running your company when the CEO isn't in the room. When they work, hard decisions become easier—not because the decisions hurt less, but because you know why you're making them.

Your Foundation never changes. Your Principles guide decisions when nobody's watching. But there's a third layer: how customers actually experience you.

5
CHARACTERISTICS

How the world experiences you—and why this must evolve.

I f the Foundation is your company's soul, and Principles are your conscience and behaviors, then Characteristics are your personality. They are the emotional and tonal traits, like being adventurous, playful, or artful, that determine how your brand shows up in the world.

Let's recap:

Foundation: What you make possible. Never changes. Michelin enables exploration. Kohler enables transformation. Amazon removes friction from customers' lives.

Principles: How you make decisions. Evolves carefully over decades. CVS evolved from convenience to health-first. Patagonia evolved from protecting climbing spots to preserving the planet.

Characteristics: This is your behavioral DNA—the emotional and tonal traits that shape how you show up. It must be carefully assessed and slightly refreshed every three to five years. This is your brand's personality, expressed through traits such as Warm, Friendly, Witty, Understated, and Unexpected. These traits inform your visual identity, tone of voice, product design language, marketing style, advertising, and every customer touchpoint, from brand and eCommerce to home delivery.

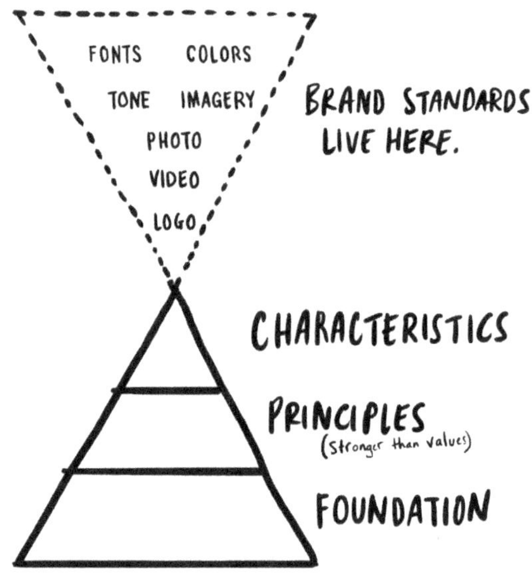

This is something many companies get wrong; they think Characteristics are the logo, the color palette, and the campaign. Those are outputs. Characteristics are the personality traits that drive those outputs. Take, for example, a fictitious leisurewear brand with one of the Principles being "Artful and Human Expressive Spirit." Their Characteristics might be:

1. Raw, Creative, DIY Energy

We are handmade, unpolished, and artist-driven. We celebrate scribbles, paint splatters, duct tape, and personal customization. We are not perfect; we are expressive.

2. Indie, Alternative, and Anti-Mainstream

We are proudly *outside* the glossy commercial world, and aligned with raw and positive bands, underground artists, skaters, and misfits. We are not polished K-pop culture.

3. Street-Level Authenticity

We are a brand you discovered, not a brand that shouts at you. We live in skate parks, small music venues, and urban art spaces. We are the opening act.

4. Art is Identity, Not Decoration

Art is not a marketing trick. Art *is* the identity—collaborations with small artists, graffiti artists, and partnerships that feel organic and community-led.

5. Approachable and Human

We are the brand for everyone: musicians, painters, teenagers, baristas, skaters, designers, outcasts, especially outcasts.

6. Soft Rebellion

We are quietly disruptive. Not "in your face," but "I'll do me." A form of gentle rebellion expressed through creativity, not confrontation.

7. Celebrate the Imperfect and Real

We embrace the scuff and the tear. We embrace signs of life and wear. We believe in the perfectly imperfect, because it tells a story.

From those Characteristics flow everything else: font choices, color palettes, photography style, retail experience, customer service voice, and marketing/advertising.

Apple does this well. The Foundation: technology that feels human—never changes. The Principle: intuitive design for premium experiences—stays constant. However, the Characteristics evolve every few years. The colorful iMacs and "Think Different" of the late '90s. The white earbuds and minimalism of the 2000s. The space-gray aesthetic and privacy-focused design of the 2010s. The environmental activism and titanium finishes of the 2020s. Each era feels distinctly different. Each one is clearly Apple. They're refreshing Characteristics while protecting the Foundation. That's the rhythm you want.[1]

Patagonia passes this test. That environmental activism, that worn-in aesthetic, and that anti-consumerist "Don't Buy This Jacket" messaging—even without the logo, you know it's Patagonia.

----

1. Interestingly, Apple doesn't seem to have changed their logo much, if at all, since founding.

Nike passes this test. That motivational energy, focus on athletes, and "Just Do It" attitude—you know it's Nike before you see the swoosh. Their voice has evolved from pure performance motivation to a deeper, more human, culturally aware voice rooted in identity, purpose, and collective courage—from Prefontaine to Kaepernick and onward.

Most companies fail this test. Remove the logo, and they're generic, or vanilla. That's when you know your Characteristics aren't actually Characteristics; they're just following design trends and calling it brand strategy. This is where companies most commonly screw up. So, let's be crystal clear about what we're talking about before we see what happens when you get it wrong.

Case Study: Burberry

In the early 2000s, Burberry faced a crisis they hadn't seen coming. British football hooligans and working-class youth—referred to as "chavs" in UK slang—adopted Burberry's signature check pattern as their uniform. Suddenly, the brand that had been synonymous with British luxury and craftsmanship had become associated with public drunkenness, football violence, and low-rent nightclubs. Celebrities stopped wearing it. Wealthy customers avoided it. Some pubs banned anyone wearing clothing with the Burberry check pattern. The brand's most distinctive output of a Characteristic—that iconic check pattern—had been hijacked by a demographic that contradicted their entire Foundation.

Burberry's Foundation was British luxury craftsmanship for people who appreciate quiet quality and heritage. Their Principles: timelessness over trend. Protect and evolve the iconic. Heritage is a strength, not an anchor. Design with British function and elegance.

Now, the check pattern plastered on everything from scarves to bikinis had become a liability, actively destroying the brand from design backward.

They could have doubled down. "This is our pattern, we're keeping it." That's what you do with Foundations—you defend them no matter what. However, this was just a design pattern.

So, they did something radical: they pretty much killed the check. Angela Ahrendts took over as CEO in 2006, working alongside creative director Christopher Bailey (who had joined Burberry in 2001), and together they repositioned the brand. They reduced the iconic check pattern to just 10% of products—down from being on nearly everything. They refocused on British heritage—trench coats, weather resistance, and understated luxury. They bought back numerous licenses to regain control. They went dark on the pattern that had defined them for decades.

When Ahrendts arrived in 2006, Burberry reported revenue of approximately $970 million USD (£740 million). By the time she left in 2014, sales had nearly tripled to over $3 billion USD (over £2 billion). The market capitalization more than tripled from £2 billion to £7 billion during her tenure.

The Foundation never changed—the quiet British craftsmanship and quality. The Principles never changed—elegance and heritage over trends. However, the way they visually expressed their Characteristics needed to die and be reborn. By the early 2010s, Burberry was cool again. It wasn't the old kind of cool. It was a new version—different aesthetic, and different customers—but still rooted in the same Foundation of British luxury and craft.

This is the hard part about a brand: sometimes you have to kill what built you to save what matters. You have to eat the donkey. The check pattern was iconic. It was recognizable. It was valuable. However, it was also destroying their Foundation, which meant it had to be removed.

Case Study: Banana Republic

Banana Republic started in 1978 as Mel and Patricia Ziegler's safari-inspired clothing company, literally sourcing authentic military surplus and travel wear. Their first catalog was hand-drawn. The stores looked like expedition outposts, complete with jeeps and jungle foliage. It was theatrical, adventurous, and authentic. They sold the romantic possibility of exploration.

Gap Inc. acquired them in 1983, and by the late 1980s, when the

Zieglers lost creative control, they had systematically stripped away everything distinctive. The hand-drawn catalogs became standard photography. The theatrical stores became standard retail. The authentic safari wear became "business casual." By the 2000s, Banana Republic was indistinguishable from every other mall brand selling the same khakis and button-downs.

Banana Republic generated $2.54 billion in sales in the fiscal year 2020. By 2021, that had collapsed to $1.46 billion—a 42% decline. Comparable store sales fell 15% in single quarters during 2015. By 2022, sales remained 15% below 2019 levels, despite two years of recovery efforts.[2]

Where did those customers go?

Fast fashion ate them alive. H&M, Zara, and Forever 21 offered similar styles at a fraction of the price. When Banana Republic charged $90 for a shirt with no clear identity, customers could get something nearly identical elsewhere. The "affordable luxury" positioning collapsed. They were too expensive to compete with fast fashion, yet too bland to justify premium pricing against brands like J. Crew or Brooks Brothers. The casualwear market actually grew during this period as workplace dress codes relaxed. But Banana Republic couldn't capture it. They'd built their identity around business casual just as business casual was dying. When the pandemic accelerated work-from-home and athleisure, their soul, and thus, core product, became obsolete.

Meanwhile, their mall locations became liabilities. As foot traffic vanished, Banana Republic couldn't pivot to e-commerce because they had no distinctive brand with which to attract digital shoppers. Why order generic khakis online from Banana Republic when Amazon offered a wider selection at better prices? They never defined the Characteristics that made those early stores work. Adventurous, authentic, worldly, crafted, and unexpected; those personality traits could have stayed constant while the visual expression evolved. They could have maintained that explorer spirit through modern design, sustainable

---

2. Women's Wear Daily, "A Repositioning Banana Republic Adds to the Mix," February 24, 2022.

materials, or artisan collaborations—a thousand ways to express "adventure and authenticity" without literal safari gear.

Instead, when corporate efficiency demanded standardization, they had nothing to protect. The outputs changed, and their Foundation disappeared. They abandoned what made them distinctive entirely, thinking the safari aesthetic was the problem, when really it was just one expression of something deeper they had failed to define.

Patagonia also sells exploration, but their Characteristics evolved from "serious climbers only" to "accessible environmental activism" while protecting the Foundation. Banana Republic just became another Gap brand selling khakis. Now they're functionally dead, kept alive only by Gap Inc.'s infrastructure.

Case Study: Dove

In 2004, Dove launched the "Real Beauty" campaign. Instead of using models, they showed real women. Instead of airbrushing, they showed stretch marks and wrinkles.

Dove's Foundation is personal care that makes people feel genuinely good about themselves. One of their Principles addresses authenticity in beauty standards. Their Characteristics—the personality traits that define how they show up—are warm, honest, human-centered, and inclusive. The "Real Beauty" campaign wasn't the Characteristic. It was those traits made visible—one specific expression of Dove's authentic, reassuring character in a culture dominated by impossible beauty standards.

Twenty years later, they're still running versions of the same campaign. It still works. The Foundation hasn't changed—helping people feel good about themselves. The Principle hasn't changed—authenticity in beauty. The character traits—warm, honest, and inclusive—remain constant. But how they express those traits has evolved with culture. What began as print ads showing diverse body types became social media movements, documentary films, and partnerships with schools, teaching self-esteem.

A campaign is not a Characteristic. Your character traits might be quiet, calm, and deep. Those traits will inform how you show up—

maybe through understated luxury, or quality pieces without logos. But the specific outfit you wear today? That's just one expression. Tomorrow, you might express the same traits differently. Dove's character traits have remained relatively stable—warm, honest, and inclusive. However, the way they express those traits evolves constantly. The "Real Beauty" campaign has worked for twenty years. When it stops working, they'll hopefully find a new expression—different ads, different message, or a different aesthetic—that still reflects their character.

Most companies struggle with Characteristics in predictable ways. Understanding these patterns helps you avoid making the same errors —and more importantly, helps you recognize it when you're already making them.

Refreshing Too Often

Every rebrand feels like starting over. The logo changes every three years. Visual identity shifts with every CMO. The tone of voice pivots. This is chaos instead of evolution.

Tropicana learned this in 2009. After decades with their iconic "straw in the orange" packaging, they refreshed to a modern, minimalist design. Sales dropped 20% in one month—a $30 million loss. Customers couldn't find their orange juice anymore. The packaging had changed so radically that Tropicana became invisible on shelves it had dominated for years. They reversed the redesign after just six weeks, but the damage was done.[3]

The problem wasn't that they refreshed—it's that they refreshed everything at once, so dramatically that they erased the memory structures customers had built over decades.

Customers can't form memory structures when you keep changing

____

3. "What to Learn from Tropicana's Packaging Redesign Failure?" The Branding Journal, May 2015.

too quickly. They no longer know who you are. Each refresh erases the investment you made in the previous one.

Instagram falls into this trap differently with constant small changes that add up to instability. The interface changes every few months. Features appear and disappear. The algorithm shifts unpredictably. Users joke that they have to relearn Instagram every quarter. This continuous churn prevents people from developing muscle memory and creates anxiety about whether their understanding of the platform will remain valid.

This is usually a symptom of not knowing your Foundation. When you're unclear about what remains constant, everything else feels negotiable. So you change constantly, hoping something sticks. You're optimizing for novelty instead of recognition.

Never Refreshing

Kodak continued to push film after digital had won. They had actually invented the digital camera in 1975, but refused to pursue it aggressively because it threatened their film business. They defended the Characteristic (film photography and the ritual of developing pictures) instead of protecting their Foundation of capturing and preserving moments. By the time they seriously tried to pivot to digital, it was too late.

Sears maintained the same catalog aesthetic into the internet age. The thick catalog that felt authoritative and comprehensive in 1985 had become a joke by 2005. They thought the catalog was what made them special, when really it was convenience and selection.

BlackBerry held 43% of the US smartphone market in 2010. By 2016, it had fallen to 0.8%.[4] Their Foundation was trusted mobile communication for professionals. Their Characteristics were precision, control, and reliability. However, they expressed those traits through a physical keyboard—and they confused the expression with the character itself.

When the iPhone arrived with a touchscreen, BlackBerry dismissed it. "No one wants a phone without a physical keyboard."

---

4. According to Comscore MobiLens reports, January 2010 and February 2016.

Precision, control, and professionalism could have been expressed differently. Apple delivered precision through touchscreen gestures, control through intuitive software, and professionalism through sleek design. The same emotional needs—different expression. BlackBerry defended how they looked instead of protecting who they were.

This is confusing Characteristics with Foundation. You think the khakis are what made you special, when really, it was accessible style. You think the film is what made you special, when really it was capturing moments. You think the catalog is what made you special, when really it was convenience. Change too often, and you create chaos. Never change, and you become irrelevant.

When I worked in advertising and brand design, clients would come in wanting a rebrand because their competitors looked more modern. "We need a new logo. We need a new color palette. We need to look like them."

However, looking like your competitor is the opposite of what you want. If you're both using the same geometric sans-serif font and the same gradient color scheme, you've become interchangeable. You've optimized your way to invisibility.

Moreover, if you spend your life obsessing over competitors, you spend less time obsessing over customers. If you obsess over customers, your business will automatically migrate forward and grow. When you obsess over competitors, you go backward. Your Characteristics should make you recognizable. Evolution and trend-chasing aren't the same thing. Character is not an ad campaign. It is the personality of the brand.

If I removed your logo from your materials, would people still recognize it as yours? If your Characteristics are strong, the answer is yes. Your voice, your visual style, and your personality should be distinctive enough that the logo is almost redundant.

In 2006, Target removed their company name from most applications entirely. Just the bullseye remained. No text. No explanation. The confidence to do this came from research showing that 96% of

Americans already recognized the bullseye as Target, making the word "Target" redundant.[5] The red and white circles alone carried all the meaning the brand needed. This was proof that their Characteristics—the playful use of the bullseye across advertising, the signature red and white color scheme, and the accessible-but-stylish positioning—had become so distinctive that the logo itself was almost unnecessary.

You need to establish a rhythm. Not a complete rebrand every time, but a meaningful refresh that demonstrates your continued cultural relevance. Think of it as updating your wardrobe—you're not becoming a different person, but you're making sure your self-expression still fits the current moment.

Your Characteristics are the easiest layer to change, which makes them dangerously easy to get wrong. Test yours right now. Show your materials to someone who is unfamiliar with your brand. Remove your logo. Can they still identify you? Can they describe your personality?

If they say "professional" or "modern," you've failed. Those are generic. You need words that only describe you.

Check for internal consistency too. Does your Instagram profile feel like a different company than your website? Does your store experience contradict your advertising voice? Inconsistency signals confusion about who you are.

Here's where things go sideways. A competitor's aesthetic gains traction, so you copy it. Design trends shift to flat minimalism, so you follow. An agency brings the same style they used for their last three clients, and you accept it. Within months, you've drifted. You didn't abandon your Characteristics consciously—you just never defended them.

Burberry killed their check pattern because it was destroying their Foundation of British craftsmanship. It was painful, but it was the right choice. They protected what mattered by sacrificing what didn't.

Banana Republic abandoned their safari identity to chase mall traffic. They thought they were evolving. Instead, they were erasing. The

---

5. According to a Target corporate study from 2003, as cited in Twin Cities Business, March 2020.

brand became generic because they changed away from their Foundation instead of changing from one expression of it to a better one.

Evolution requires intention. You refresh Characteristics in service of your Foundation. You don't drift toward safety, follow trends, or copy whoever looks successful this quarter. Foundations never change. Principles evolve when they must, and you have to manage this carefully. Characteristics refresh regularly—but only so you can express your Foundation more clearly, not so that you abandon it.

6

THE TWO STATES

Why every company exists in either Explorer or Static mode.

We've established the Foundation—your unchanging roots. Now, let's talk about the seasons: the inescapable rhythm of growth. Every company, every team, and every person exists in one of two states right now: Static (optimizing what exists) or Explorer (discovering what doesn't). Don't treat states as permanent identities. I'm going to show you how to read the hidden signals that reveal which state you're actually in, and why mastering the transition between them is the core of competitive survival.

In 2012, Best Buy was dying, but they knew it before anyone else did. Store traffic was up. People were walking through doors, spending time in aisles, picking up products, and asking questions. The dashboards glowed green. But sales were flat. Conversion was dropping.

The hidden reality: customers were using Best Buy as Amazon's showroom—examining products in person before buying them online for a lower price. They'd spend twenty minutes with a sales associate learning about cameras, then pull out their phone and order it on Amazon while still standing in the aisle.

Many companies would have waited and gathered more data. Run more studies. Built the perfect case until the trend was undeniable to everyone, including their competitors. By then, the shift would have become traumatic rather than deliberate. By then, you've lost the muscle memory for exploration.

Best Buy's CEO, Hubert Joly, made a different choice.

He recognized that Best Buy was stuck in a Static State—optimizing store layouts, perfecting inventory systems, and tweaking their existing model. They needed to shift to Explorer State, and they needed to do it while they were still profitable, still had energy, and still had options.

Instead of fighting the showrooming trend or pretending it wasn't happening, Joly accepted that the world had changed: Best Buy was now competing with Amazon inside their own stores. So he transformed Best Buy into both Amazon's competitor and partner—offering price matching, same-day delivery, and even becoming a distribution point for other retailers. They turned their biggest weakness into their greatest strength.

The company that was supposed to be the next Circuit City is still here. Not because they had a better strategy, but because they understood the rhythm. They knew when to shift states, and they made it a choice rather than a crisis.

In statistics, there's a concept called a Hidden Markov Model. The actual state of reality is hidden—you can't observe it directly. However, you can observe signals—outputs that hint at what's happening beneath the surface.

You can't see the future, but the patterns tell you something. You can't see the wind, but you can watch the trees bend. You can't see what customers are really thinking. You can't see where the market is heading. You can't see what your culture truly believes. These are hidden states. Nevertheless, you can observe signals that reveal the hidden reality.

A sudden spike in customer service calls about a feature you thought was minor? That's a signal. Three of your best people leaving in six months for "new opportunities"? That's your organization broadcasting its hidden state. Your social media engagement is dropping while follower count stays steady? That's people quietly tuning you out. Returns increasing even as sales hold steady? Customers are trying you and rejecting you.

Best Buy's initial metrics—healthy foot traffic—was a signal that suggested everything was fine. But conversion rates dropping, and average transaction value declining were different signals, revealing a hidden state of customers using stores for research but buying elsewhere.

Don't just look for the signals you want to see. Look at all of them, even—especially—the uncomfortable ones. Start by looking for pattern breaks, not data points. One bad review isn't a signal. One employee leaving isn't a signal. However, when something that's been consistent for years suddenly changes—that's worth investigating. When customer satisfaction scores decline for six consecutive quarters after years of growth, something fundamental has shifted.

Then track what people do, not what they say. Customers will tell you your product is "interesting" and never buy it. Employees will say morale is "fine" while updating their LinkedIn profiles. What people say is optimized for politeness. What they do reveals the truth.

Pay attention to what's not being said. The meetings where a critical topic isn't mentioned. The Slack channels that have gone quiet. The questions that stopped coming because people had already decided what the answer was. Sometimes the signal is absence.

You also need to measure second-order effects, not just first-order metrics. Revenue tells you whether people are buying. Customer acquisition cost relative to lifetime value tells you whether your business model is sustainable. Employee retention tells you whether people are staying. The quality of who's leaving versus who's staying tells you whether your culture is broken.

Most importantly, create systems to bring uncomfortable truths to the surface. Our brains filter out data that contradicts what we want to believe. The only defense is building truth-telling into your systems. Do junior employees feel safe challenging senior leaders? Do your dashboards show what's declining or just what's growing? Do your retrospectives examine failures honestly or just check a box?

The companies that read signals well have built truth-telling into their systems. The companies that miss signals have built comfort into theirs.

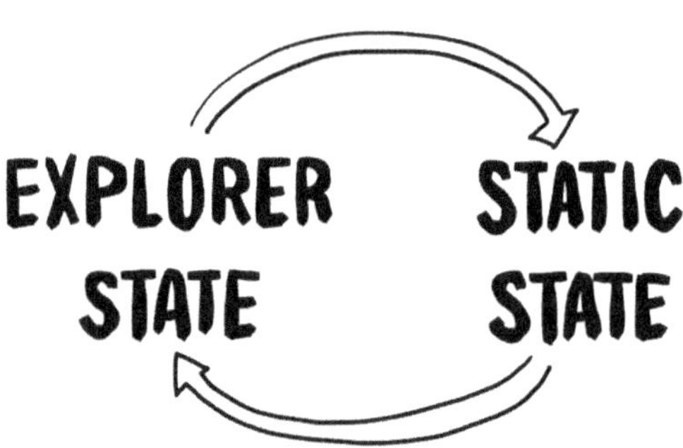

Every company exists in one of two states at any given moment.

Static State is when you're optimizing what exists—making your current model more efficient, your products better, and your processes smoother. This isn't bad. It's essential. Static State generates the profits that let you take risks. It builds the capabilities you'll leverage later. It funds exploration.

However, Static State has a shelf life. The world doesn't stop changing just because you've perfected your business model. Every quarter you spend optimizing is a quarter someone else spends exploring. Eventually, perfection becomes obsolescence.

Explorer State is when you're discovering what doesn't exist yet—probing new markets, testing new capabilities, and building new muscle. Explorer State creates your future. It finds the opportunities that will matter when your current model stops working.

However, you can't stay in Explorer State forever. People burn out. Resources deplete. You need time to consolidate what you've learned, to build systems around what works, and to recover before the next push.

Here's the mistake: companies treat these as permanent identities instead of temporary conditions.

"We're an innovation company," they announce, while burning through talent and capital without ever building anything that lasts.

"We're a performance-driven company," they declare, while optimizing themselves into irrelevance.

You're not either. You're both. The question is which state you need right now and how long you should stay there.

The Static State follows a predictable pattern:

1. Success breeds complacency. You find something that works. Customers love it. Revenue grows. Margins expand. You naturally want to protect and optimize this success.
2. Optimization becomes religion. You hire consultants to make your successful thing more efficient. You create processes to ensure consistency. You develop metrics to track performance. You eliminate variations that might disrupt the formula.
3. Risk becomes unacceptable. Why experiment when the current model works? Why explore new territories when you're profitable in your current one? The organization develops antibodies against anything that threatens the status quo.
4. The world changes, you don't. A new technology emerges. Customer preferences shift. A competitor tries something different. But you're so locked into your optimized model that adaptation feels impossible.
5. Collapse. What seemed like a strong, stable business can suddenly no longer compete. Your optimized processes are perfectly designed for a world that no longer exists.

~

I learned about this pattern while I was working at Publicis. I was reviewing budgets with the CFO, looking at our 23% margins. I was proud of those numbers.

"That margin is too high," he told me.

I didn't understand. How can profit be too high?

"When margins get fat, thinking gets lazy," he explained. "You stop investing in capabilities. You stop taking risks. You optimize for extraction instead of creation. Then, when markets shift—and they always shift—you have no resilience. No new capabilities. No plan B."

He walked me through what happens when margins climb too high:

You stop investing in training. Why spend money developing people when current skills are generating profit? The team stops learning new capabilities because the old ones still work. You stop following the customer—really following them, understanding where they're going next, and what they'll need in two years. Instead, you continue to follow your existing business, squeezing more efficiency from what you already know.

You stop growing the team. Why add headcount when margins prove you're overstaffed for current demand? However, this means that, when opportunities emerge, you lack the capacity to pursue them. When markets shift, you don't have people who understand the new territory. You stop experimenting. Why risk margin compression testing new approaches when the current model delivers? So you keep optimizing yesterday's business model while tomorrow's opportunity passes by.

This is what creates the opening for disruption. When Western Union maintained fat margins for decades, charging high fees to send money internationally, they created vulnerability. Remitly saw resident workers sending money home to families in neighboring countries—families that often lacked banking options—and built an app that undercut Western Union's pricing dramatically.

Remitly's entire strategy could have been summarized as: "Their margin is our opportunity."

That's the risk of stagnant stability. Your profitable efficiency becomes someone else's market entry point.

When you're truly following the customer—really adapting to where they're going—you automatically learn and grow. Every adaptation builds new capability. Every shift develops new muscles. But when money is tight, or margins are fat, you follow what you already know. You protect what you have rather than building what you need. At that point, you're not progressing. You're static. And when you're static, other companies progress. This means you're not standing still—you're moving backward. You're declining.

That Publicis CFO showed me companies that had maintained 30% margins for years, only to disappear overnight when their market changed. They'd extracted all the value and built nothing new. They had perfected yesterday's business model right into bankruptcy. When the markets shifted—and markets continually shift—they had nothing to fall back on. No new capabilities. No new relationships. No understanding of where customers were heading.

Most CEOs would kill for 30% margins. However, those margins are often a symptom of the Static State, not success. You're extracting value from past innovations rather than investing in future ones. You're harvesting rather than planting. And when the harvest runs out, you will discover that you forgot to plant seeds for next season.

Case Study: Under Armour

In 2015, Under Armour was unstoppable. Revenue had grown for 26 consecutive quarters. Their market cap hit $20 billion. Kevin Plank declared they would surpass Nike. Every visible metric pointed up.

However, Plank misread what moment they were in. After years of successful growth in an Explorer State—inventing moisture-wicking fabric, launching "Protect This House," and creating new categories of athletic wear—Under Armour desperately needed a Static State period. They needed to consolidate operations, strengthen their Foundation, and turn exploration into excellence.

At that time, I was embedded in growth sporting brands within the LVMH portfolio. Every brand I touched had phenomenal Foundations

—they were founder-led—and their task was to be the next Under Armour. Several ex-Under Armour employees were on the team. The energy of Plank, and his passion, were palpable. He was the brand.

However, even the best leaders need to operate in both modes. Effective CEOs don't choose between exploration and optimization— they enable both simultaneously through their teams. One segment focuses on protecting what works while another explores what's next. Some leaders drive this through competing tracks, setting up parallel teams pursuing different strategies. Others simply ensure their leadership team is explicitly designed for both Explorer and Static activities at the same time.

Plank never created this balance. He kept exploring without discipline, and his entire organization followed his lead. He saw Dick's Sporting Goods expanding and pivoted heavily into wholesale distribution. He saw Nike's FuelBand and raced to join that market by acquiring fitness apps for $710 million. He saw Lululemon's lifestyle positioning and pushed into fashion. He was chasing whatever competitors were doing instead of protecting what made Under Armour distinctive. Plan abandoned his Foundation (solving real problems for seriously competitive athletes) and his Characteristics (earned performance, relentless drive, and functional innovation) to chase trends that had nothing to do with his brand's DNA.

Under Armour was built on earned performance and relentless drive—not fashion as lifestyle. The fitness apps had millions of users and generated data, but they violated Under Armour's Foundation: athletes didn't need another app tracking their workouts. They needed better gear that helped them perform. The apps were exploration without purpose—expensive distractions from what Under Armour actually did well.

Meanwhile, their core business was crying out for Static State excellence. Athletes noticed product quality declining while Under Armour chased after shiny new objects. Distribution needed optimization while executives acquired random companies. Their most profitable product, the famous UA hoodie, was forgotten. The Foundation required reinforcement while leadership chased competitors.

By 2017, reality hit. Revenue stalled. The stock crashed from $52 to

$10. They'd failed at both states—neither consolidating their victories, nor exploring strategically.

Compare this to Lululemon, which mastered the rhythm for years. They'd explore (new fabrics, and new categories), then consolidate (perfect the product, and optimize operations), then explore again (men's lines, lifestyle products), always from their Foundation of technical athletic apparel for yoga and training. Clear cycles, and deliberate transitions, never confusing motion with progress.

Until they didn't.

By late 2024, Lululemon's stock had dropped 50%. The brand that had once owned "premium yoga-focused athleisure for women who valued wellness culture" was scrambling. They launched NFL-branded Align leggings and Scuba hoodies through Fanatics—slapping team logos on existing products to access 140 million NFL fans.

This was Under Armour's playbook. Different tactics, same disease. Lululemon licensed NFL logos that accessed massive audiences but dilute their Foundation. Both are borrowing relevance instead of building it. Both confused motion with progress.

When you need another brand's equity to make your product relevant, you have a positioning crisis.

Under Armour's market cap fell to $3.4 billion—down 80% from its peak. Lululemon sits at $38 billion, but is falling. The brand that was supposed to be the cautionary tale's opposite is now following the same path—just more slowly.

I'll be honest: throughout this book, I lean heavily on Explorer State examples. They're dramatic. They show transformation. They feel like the hero's journey of business. But that emphasis comes with a warning—you can kill a company by staying in either state too long.

Under Armour proves what happens when you never shift into Static State to protect what you built. But the opposite is just as deadly. Stay in Static State too long and you get comfortable. Each day makes it harder to move. If you sit on the couch binge-watching television and eating peanut M&Ms for too long, you'll get fat, and each day that passes makes it harder to get back on your feet. Similarly, when you stay static in work and business too long, it gets harder and harder to see a path back to Explorer State. The muscle atrophies. The organization forgets how to change.

Both states are essential. The rhythm between them is essential. Plank kept exploring without discipline, and his entire organization followed his lead.

~

The Static State is the opposite of chaos. It's a condition of continuous refinement where the goal isn't to discover what's new but to perfect what already works.

Static organizations share specific Characteristics that Explorer organizations find limiting:

They cultivate productive stability. Not all stability is equal. There's stagnant stability that calcifies organizations. Then there's productive stability that compounds expertise.

In general, Static organizations reward people who have answers, whereas Explorer organizations reward people who ask questions no one else is asking. Trail runners have a saying that refers to the first person on that trail that morning; they are "breaking cobwebs." Running through spider webs that formed overnight. Breaking trails means being the first person there ever. Explorer State is about breaking trails.

Organizations in a Static phase reward people who have the right answers. "Here's the proven approach" becomes more valuable than "What if we tried something different?"

They measure execution excellence over learning velocity. Instead of tracking how quickly they adapt to new information, they track how consistently they deliver known results. How precisely can they replicate success? How efficiently can they scale proven processes? How many quality standards are they maintaining simultaneously?

They protect focus time religiously. While Explorer companies encourage exploration and experimentation, companies in the Static phase understand that mastery happens through deep, uninterrupted work on core competencies.

I've seen teams lose entire quarters to "innovation theater"—

running workshops, brainstorming sessions, and exploring possibilities—when what they really needed was six months of heads-down execution. You can't build expertise by constantly context-switching. If your team is in a different strategic direction every quarter, you're not innovating—you're just thrashing about.

They hire for proven competence over potential. Curiosity can lead anywhere. Experience leads somewhere specific. Static organizations need people who've already mastered the fundamentals, who know the industry deeply, and who can execute without supervision. McKinsey's interview questions reveal this priority. They ask, "Walk me through a complex analysis you've completed." "Describe how you would structure this specific business problem." "What frameworks would you apply to this case?"

Notice what they're not asking about: times you failed and learned, situations where you invented something new, or examples of unconventional thinking. They're asking about rigor, structure, and proven methodologies—the hard skills that determine whether someone can deliver excellence consistently.

The Explorer State is the opposite of optimization. It's a condition of continuous discovery where the goal isn't to perfect what exists but to find what doesn't yet exist.

Organizations in an Explorer phase share specific Characteristics that Static organizations find wasteful:

They cultivate productive discomfort. Not all discomfort is equal. There's destructive discomfort that breaks people and organizations. Then there's productive discomfort that builds capability. Explorer organizations know the difference.

They value questions over answers. Static organizations reward people who have answers. Explorer organizations reward people who ask questions no one else is asking. "Why does it have to be this way?" becomes more valuable than "Here's how we've always done it."

They measure learning velocity over efficiency. Instead of tracking how well they execute known processes, they track how quickly they can adapt to new information. How fast can they detect market shifts?

How rapidly can they pivot strategies? How many experiments are running simultaneously?

They protect thinking time religiously. While Static companies pack calendars and measure productivity by meetings attended, Explorer companies understand that breakthrough thinking happens in the spaces between activities.

I'm booked from 7:30 AM to 6PM most days—zero time to think. And if you want great creative work, you have to allow teams the time to think and process. But they don't have it because they have to fill out timesheets. If you put 40 hours a week down to "thinking," you can imagine the outcry—but without a certain amount of that time, you're not exploring—you're just executing faster.

They hire for curiosity over competence. Technical skills can be taught. Industry experience can be gained. But curiosity—genuine, relentless, and sometimes annoying curiosity—is either there or it isn't. Amazon's interview questions reveal this priority. They ask, "Tell me about a time you took ownership of a project outside your job description." "Describe a situation where you had to make a decision with incomplete information." "Give an example of when you simplified a complex process or invented a new approach."

Notice what they're not asking about: specific software tools, years of experience in the industry, or technical certifications. They're asking about judgment, curiosity, and ownership—the soft skills that determine whether someone will raise the bar or lower it.

Case Study: Adidas

Bjørn Gulden walked into Adidas in January 2023, facing massive headwinds. The company had just cut ties with Kanye West, leaving $1.3 billion in Yeezy inventory sitting in warehouses. Revenue for 2022 had been $23.7 billion, but operating profit had plummeted 66% to $708 million. North America sales were collapsing.[1]

The core problem: it was taking twelve months to approve a shoe design. By the time Adidas brought a product to market, competitors

---

1. Adidas AG financial reports, 2022-2023; Retail Insight Network, March 2023.

had already released three versions. Decision-making required multiple committee approvals, each adding weeks to the process. Product managers presented to directors, who presented to VPs, who presented to committees, who made recommendations to other committees.

Gulden eliminated entire management layers overnight. Not a restructuring—a demolition. Teams that had previously needed seventeen approvals now controlled their own budgets and decisions. Product managers who'd spent careers seeking consensus suddenly owned outcomes completely. No safety nets. No committees to distribute blame. Just ownership.

The transformation was immediate and brutal. Some managers couldn't function without approval structures. They'd been trained to minimize personal risk, not make decisions. However, others thrived. Teams started moving like startups inside the corporation. What had taken months now took weeks.

The Yeezy crisis demanded immediate action. While competitors expected Adidas to dump inventory at fire-sale prices, Gulden sold it at cost and donated $160 million to anti-racism organizations. One decision. No committees. No months of analysis. The PR disaster became a redemption story.

Then Gulden abandoned the celebrity strategy entirely. While Nike and competitors fought over endorsement deals, he returned to the Samba and Gazelle—shoes that had generated profits for forty years without celebrity association. Classic designs. Proven demand. No drama. The Foundation wasn't celebrity culture. The Foundation was athletic performance.

He cut $1.7 billion in bloated inventory, eliminated lifestyle collaborations that diluted the brand, partnered with actual athletes instead of influencers, and simplified operations across all regions. Everything focused on one thing: making Adidas "a machine again." Not a fashion house. Not a lifestyle brand. A machine that produces great athletic products.

Two years later, operating profit surged to $1.4 billion in 2024—up from just $292 million in 2023. Revenue climbed 12% to $25.5 billion.

Adidas stock outperformed Nike and Puma, rising 66% since Gulden took over. The projected 2025 operating profit is $1.9 billion.[2]

No layoffs. No bailouts. No asset sales. No emergency capital. Just structural transformation.

The twelve-month approval process hadn't been about quality control. It was organizational scar tissue—every layer added after some previous failure, every committee created to prevent some past mistake. Process had become the product. Structure had become the strategy. The company was optimizing its own decline.

Gulden forced Adidas from Static State to Explorer State through organizational violence. He didn't inspire change. He made the old way impossible. When your only choice is to move fast or fail, most people learn to move fast.

Are you in the state that your organization needs right now?

If you've been optimizing the same model for five years, you're probably overdue for exploration. If you've been exploring for five years without building anything lasting, you're probably overdue for consolidation.

However, you can't just declare, "We're now in Explorer State" and expect it to happen. States aren't chosen through PowerPoint decks or all-hands meetings. They're built through systems, incentives, and leadership behavior.

Signals you've been Static too long:

Your best people are leaving for "new challenges." When your talent starts talking about wanting to learn and grow somewhere else, that's about you. You've optimized away the interesting problems. You've made everything so efficient, so predictable, and so comfortable that there's nothing left to explore. Denzel Washington said it perfectly:

---

2. Adidas AG Annual Reports, 2023-2024; Sportico, April 2025.

"Ease is a greater threat to progress than hardship."[3] Your comfortable efficiency is exactly what's driving your best people away.

Simple decisions require complex processes. When it takes three meetings and four approvals to change something that should take thirty minutes, you've built scar tissue. Every process you've added to prevent old failures is now preventing new success. You've optimized for risk avoidance rather than progress. That ease of never making mistakes? That is exactly what is killing your ability to move forward.

Competitors are competing on dimensions you don't understand. They're not trying to beat you at your game. They're playing a different game entirely, and you're still perfecting the wrong playbook. While you were getting comfortable optimizing your existing model, they were out in the discomfort of building something new. Your ease became their opportunity.

Signals you're exploring without purpose:

You can't explain the connection between your explorations and your Foundation. When someone asks why you're pursuing a project and the answer is, "It seemed like a good opportunity" rather than "It strengthens our Foundation," you're wandering.

Projects die from neglect rather than decision. Initiatives fade away without clear endings. People move on to new explorations before finishing current ones. This isn't strategic exploration—it's attention deficit disorder.

Resources are spread so thin that nothing gets enough to succeed. When you're funding twelve explorations at 20% each instead of three at 80%, you've confused activity with progress.

You're exhausted but can't point to what you've built. If everyone's working 60-hour weeks and you can't articulate what capabilities or products you've created, you're burning energy without building capacity.

Understanding the states isn't enough. You need to master the rhythm between them.

This brings us to the next question: if states are temporary, what

---

3. Denzel Washington, acceptance speech at the 48th NAACP Image Awards, February 11, 2017.

stays constant? If you're constantly shifting between Explorer and Static phases, what keeps you from losing yourself entirely?

Your Foundation is what you are. The states are just where you are in the cycle. Master the rhythm between states while protecting your Foundation, and you can transform things without losing yourself.

Lose sight of your Foundation while shifting between states, and you become whatever the market wants you to be—which is usually nothing in particular.

7
THE RHYTHM

Mastering the transitions between growth and consolidation.

My friend Nathan packed up his car and his dog and drove from California to Brazil. It took him two years to get to his destination. Not just because the route was complicated (which it was), but because he understood that you don't take a journey like that solely to arrive somewhere. You take it to become someone different.

Nathan was choosing his donkey moments, the deliberate hardships you put yourself through because you know comfort doesn't create capability. Athletes understand this. You don't run a triathlon because it's pleasant. You run it because the person who finishes is different from the person who started. Companies expanding to new markets, launching new products, or rebuilding their culture—they're all eating their version of the donkey. They're choosing the productive discomfort that builds what comfort never could.

You can't stay uncomfortable forever, but you can't stay comfortable forever either. You need both. The rhythm between them is what makes growth sustainable.

For weeks at a time, Nathan would be in pure Explorer State—

driving day after day through Mexico, Belize, and Guatemala. Everything was unfamiliar. Every day was uncomfortable. He was sleeping in strange towns, eating whatever he could find, pushing constantly south. The discomfort was productive—he was covering ground, discovering new territories, and building resilience. Every day changed him slightly. Every challenge built a new capability.

Then he'd stop. In Santa Marta for four months. Cuenca for four weeks. Lima for six weeks. Buenos Aires for six months.

He'd settle down for a while without losing sight of the long-term adventure. During these stops, he'd go to the same coffee shop every morning. He'd eat at the same restaurant three nights in a row. He'd do his laundry, and call his mom. These weren't failures of adventure—they were what made the adventure possible. This was his Static State, and he needed it to recover, to process what he'd learned, and to consolidate the person he was becoming.

You don't digest donkey meat while you're eating it. You digest it in the quiet moments after. You integrate what you learned. You let your body adapt to what you put it through. You prepare for the next arduous push by resting from the last one.

Then, after weeks of comfort, the itch would return. The rental home would feel like a cage. The familiar restaurant would taste boring. The Static State would have done its job—restored him, and consolidated his growth—and now staying still would mean declining. So he'd pack up and dive back into the unknown.

This is the rhythm every company needs, but few master: knowing when to choose your donkey moment, and when to stop and digest what you learned from it. When to push into productive discomfort and when to consolidate in temporary stability. When to explore and when to optimize. Not because either state is better, but because growth only happens through the oscillation between them.

Stay in the Explorer State, and you burn out. You explore without ever building anything lasting from your discoveries. Stay in the Static State, and you decay. You optimize yesterday's success until the market moves on without you.

Deliberately choose your moments of productive discomfort. Strategically consolidate what you learned. That's how you build something that endures. Comfort and discomfort aren't opposites; they're partners. This is how companies grow: not through perpetual exploration or permanent stability, but through mastering the rhythm between them.

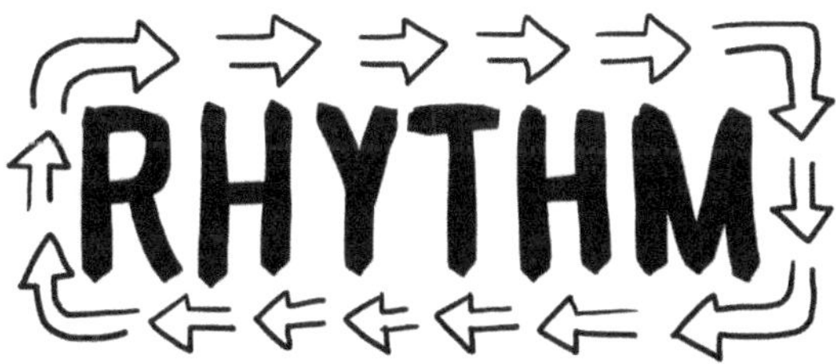

Companies fail at rhythm because they confuse the temporary state with permanent identity. They think they're "an explorer" or "an optimizer" when they should be thinking, "We're in Explorer State right now" or "We're in Static State right now."

The Static State is comfortable. You know what you're doing. The metrics are predictable. Shareholders are happy. Employees have routines. There's no obvious reason to disrupt what's working.

Until it stops working, and by then, you've lost the muscle memory for exploration. Your best explorers have left. Your processes have calcified. Your culture has forgotten how to be uncomfortable. The shift from Static to Explorer becomes traumatic rather than natural.

The Explorer State is exciting. You're building the future, taking risks, and feeling alive. There's always another territory to explore, another capability to build, or another opportunity to pursue. Until you burn out. By then, you've never built the systems that turn exploration into a sustainable business. Your discoveries remain discoveries. Your capabilities remain potential. The shift from Explorer to Static feels like giving up rather than consolidating gains.

Companies that master rhythm understand that both transitions are dangerous—and necessary. Moving from Static to Explorer feels like abandoning everything that made you successful. The systems that generated profits for years suddenly feel like constraints. The processes that ensured quality suddenly feel like bureaucracy. The careful approach that protected margins suddenly feels like cowardice.

This is the transition you see when a new executive is hired—and executives are almost always hired when a team has gone Static. It's obvious to everyone except the people inside. The board sees stagnation. The new CMO sees opportunity. The existing team sees their world ending. The new executive will always employ new people. They'll try to shift the team from a Static State to a growth state. The team becomes uncomfortable. Turnover spikes. People who thrived in the old system suddenly can't perform in the new one. Those who love predictability rebel against the chaos.

This feels terrible. But it's working exactly as it should.

Among the top 100 advertisers in the United States, CMO tenure averages just 37.2 months—about three years.[1] That means the average major brand completely turns over its marketing leadership every three years because brands need the transition from Static back to Explorer. Every three years, your brand gets shocked back into motion. New leadership. New priorities. New discomfort. High turnover. It feels like failure, but it's actually the rhythm working—companies cycling between consolidation and exploration, whether they plan to or not.

The problem comes when boards panic during the discomfort. "Why would we risk what's working?" becomes the default objection. The metrics still look fine. The shareholders are happy. Revenue is growing, even if margins are compressing. So they fire the new executive before the transition is completed, hire someone to "stabilize," and drift back into Static. They mistake the productive discomfort of transition for destructive chaos.

However, the hidden state is already shifting. Your best people are leaving. Simple decisions are requiring complex processes. Your rival are competing in dimensions you don't understand. By the time these

---

1. Spencer Stuart, "CMO Tenure Study," April 2024.

signals become obvious, the shift from Static to Explorer has already become traumatic rather than natural.

Moving from Explorer to Static feels like giving up before you've finished. The experiments that generated excitement suddenly need to become systems. The flexibility that enabled discovery suddenly needs to become consistency. The chaos that felt productive suddenly needs to become organized.

This transition exhausts teams. "We're just hitting our stride!" becomes the rallying cry. There's always another territory to explore, another capability to build, or another opportunity to pursue. The energy is high, even if the exhaustion is real. But you can't stay in full-on Explorer State forever.

This is why the three-year CMO cycle matters. The executives who successfully make the Static-to-Explorer transition often can't complete the Explorer-to-Static consolidation. They're explorers, not optimizers. So after three years of pushing growth, they leave for the next challenge—and ideally, the company hires someone who can consolidate what was discovered.

The rhythm works when companies understand that both transitions are necessary. Discomfort can be progress. You have to transition deliberately, or otherwise let market forces traumatize you into it.

Foundation Theory is about maintaining your Foundation through both Explorer and Static States.

Your Foundation is what never changes. For Amazon, it's customer obsession. For Michelin, it's enabling exploration. For Kohler, it's graciousness and transformation of spaces. This stays constant regardless of which state you're in.

Your Principles guide decisions in both states. They're how you make choices when you're not in the room. These rarely change, but when they do, it's through deliberate choice, not drift.

Your Characteristics are what shift with the states. When you're in Explorer State, you might look scrappy, experimental, or chaotic. When you're in Static State, you might look polished, systematic, and controlled. Both can be authentic expressions of the same Foundation.

The companies that die have lost this clarity. They confuse their Characteristics with their Foundation. When they shift from Explorer to Static, they think they're abandoning who they are. When they shift from Static to Explorer, they think they're becoming someone new.

You're not. You're the same company, with the same Foundation, operating in a different state because that's what the moment requires. This is why Foundation clarity is the prerequisite for rhythm mastery. Without knowing what never changes, every transition feels like an identity crisis.

Watch Porsche, and you see rhythm mastery at the organizational level.

For sixty years, they've been making the 911. Same basic design. Same "wrong" rear-engine configuration. The same distinctive silhouette that every wind tunnel in the world says should be changed. However, they never confuse their Foundation with their state.

In Explorer State, they're relentless. Active aerodynamics that deploy at speed to counteract lift. Sophisticated suspension systems to manage unusual weight distribution. Hybrid powertrains. Electric variants. They explore every technology that might enhance the 911 without changing what makes it a 911.

In Static State, they optimize like German engineers obsessed with perfection. Production efficiency. Quality control. Supply chain management. They make the 911 profitably at scale, funding the exploration that keeps it relevant.

Through both states, the Foundation never changes. Rear engine. Distinctive shape. The feeling that comes from physics that shouldn't work but does. Everything else adapts.

Notice what's happening: Porsche isn't choosing between Explorer and Static. They're operating in both simultaneously in different parts of the organization. The engineering team explores new technologies while the manufacturing team optimizes production. The design studio experiments with interior materials while the supply chain team negotiates volume discounts.

When they're exploring new technologies, they're asking: does this make the 911 more of what it already is? When they're optimizing production, they're asking: does this let us protect the essentials while improving efficiency?

The Foundation makes both states possible. Without it, exploration becomes random wandering. Without it, optimization converges toward whatever everyone else is doing.

This is the advantage of clarity about your Foundation. You can have different parts of your organization in different states, moving at different speeds, exploring different territories—as long as they're all building from the same cast iron core.

Amazon demonstrates rhythm mastery at scale.

Amazon retail lives mostly in a Static State. They've spent twenty years optimizing fulfillment, perfecting logistics, and eliminating friction. This generates massive cash flow. However, they're not trying to reinvent retail fundamentals—they're trying to make retail fundamentals so efficient that no competitor can match them.

AWS lives mostly in Explorer State. When they started, they were discovering whether cloud computing could even be a business. They're still discovering—new services, new capabilities, and new markets. Some fail spectacularly. Most of what they try doesn't work.

Through everything, there is one Foundation: customer obsession. It doesn't matter which state they're in, and it doesn't matter which part of the business. The question is always the same: does this reduce friction for customers?

Most companies can't do this. They don't have the Foundation clarity to operate in multiple states simultaneously. So they lurch— everyone explores together, then everyone optimizes together. They waste years in states they don't need to be in because they can't differentiate between temporary conditions and permanent identity.

Ask yourself: when was the last time we deliberately shifted states?

If the answer is "when we were forced to," you're reactive. If the answer is "never consciously," you're drifting. If the answer is "we shift when signals indicate it's time," you're managing rather than being managed by your states.

Depending on the situation, sometimes optimization is exactly what you need.

Early in my time at Kohler, I studied how luxury brands presented their products online. Tiffany made a silver bracelet look like it belonged in a museum. Meanwhile, Kohler's products showed up inconsistently on owned and partner websites. In my opinion, Kohler also had a scale problem: 30,000 products, even more images showing up without a consistent and premium look and feel. In any company, you'd need an army of photographers and a budget that would make the CFO panic to reshoot everything traditionally.

A different approach to optimizing was required, so a gaming engine was used to re-render all of the product imagery.

Projects like this normally take about a year and a half to get right, and another year to roll out completely. And a full team with fortitude and conviction. Today's technology makes it possible to show the craftsmanship of any product: deep basins with rulers showing scale, bright finishes in proper lighting, and installation contexts that make sense.

Also, today you can quickly assess conversion lift across retail platforms to ensure the idea actually works.

That's the difference between productive optimization and the convergence cascade. A decision not to optimize toward mediocrity like everyone else. Not trying to make your imagery look like your competitors. Simple, trying to show what was already built. All to a brand's standards, and all with the same consistency.

This is what productive optimization looks like: it makes you better at being yourself. It funds exploration instead of replacing it.

In businesses, you need both optimization and brand-new thinking. The problem is that we're asking the same people to do both. That's a recipe for disaster. The person who can optimize your product imagery isn't necessarily the person who can reimagine what a bathroom means. And that's fine. You need both. Just don't get the two mixed up.

Shift proactively. Explore while you're still profitable. Optimize while you still have energy. Make the transition a choice rather than a crisis response. However, proactive shifting requires brutal honesty about where you actually are.

Are we optimizing what needs to be explored? Are we exploring what should be optimized? Are we in the right state for what we're trying to achieve? Are we protecting our Foundation in both states? Companies can't answer these questions because they've never distinguished between their temporary state and their permanent identity. They are what they're doing rather than doing what serves who they are.

Rhythm means knowing what moves and what stays fixed. Balance implies that both states are equal. They're not. You need just enough Static to fund the Explorer—and just enough comfort to enable the next discomfort. Just enough stability from which to launch.

Companies endure by mastering the rhythm between states while never forgetting their Foundation. They know when to eat the donkey and when to digest it. When to be terrible at most things so they can be extraordinary at what matters.

The rhythm? Knowing what moves and what stays fixed—what's temporary and what's permanent.

Your Foundation is permanent. Your states are temporary. Master this distinction, and you can transform without losing yourself, evolve without forgetting who you are, and explore without abandoning your core.

Call it rhythm, not balance. And rhythm, unlike balance, creates momentum.

8

PRODUCTIVE DISCOMFORT

The difference between pain that builds and pain that destroys.

Every year, companies send out employee satisfaction surveys. And every year, they get the same predictable results. People want their bosses to treat them well. They don't want to work too hard. They want a better work-life balance. All the usual stuff that sounds reasonable on a survey, but falls apart when you actually think about it.

Is our job to make people happy, or is our job to make people better? There's a big difference between the two.

I've got a recommendation on my LinkedIn profile from a guy named Erik Hostetler. We worked together at two different jobs. The last line of the recommendation says, "He makes you proud of the work you do, no matter what that work is." But in the lines before that, it says things like: "Pushes buttons? Check. Drives you crazy at least once a week? Check."

Erik understood that my job wasn't to make him comfortable. My job was to push him just enough that he'd do work he didn't think he was capable of doing. And he did. Not because of me—but because he had the talent and drive all along. I just created the productive discomfort that helped him realize it. Since then, Erik's had some of the highest positions at advertising agencies, and that's all him. I'm proud we worked together when we did.

Companies think they must choose between comfort and productivity. Employee satisfaction or business results. Happy workers or hard workers. That choice doesn't exist.

I ran Ironman races for years. Most people think endurance sports are about suffering constantly. They're not. They're about understanding the rhythm between suffering and recovery. When I was training, four or five times out of ten, you'd absolutely hate it. You'd hate getting up at 4 AM for a twenty-mile run before work. You'd be staring at the ceiling, dreading your alarm.

Maybe three times out of ten, the training was fine—not great, but not terrible. You showed up, you did the work, and you went home. Adequate. But you lived for that one to three times out of ten when it was just euphoric. When you're riding with a group, and everything clicks. When you finish a long run, and you're walking on air, feeling invincible. When you feel that runner's high, it makes you remember why you do this.

Business is exactly the same. Some days are hard. Some days are fine. But you need those euphoric days—when you ship something great, when a campaign performs beyond expectations, or when the team rallies and creates magic. Those days happen because of the work you put in on the hard days.

Optimize out all discomfort, and you'll have teams that can't handle pressure. Grind people into dust, and you'll get burnout and turnover. Neither extreme works. What works is rhythm. Knowing when to push and when to recover.

Some discomfort creates growth. Some creates resentment, burnout, and quiet quitting. Productive discomfort—the kind that actually makes people and companies better—follows specific patterns.

Rule 1: It Must Be Consensual

When someone on my team asks for a promotion, I lay out what it takes. They look at the list and say, "That's a lot."

I tell them: "One day, someone on your team is going to ask you for a promotion. My job is to make sure you're ready for that conversation."

Then I shut up. They can walk away. Nobody's forcing anything.

By contrast, grind culture where people work eighty-hour weeks because "that's just how it is here" is just exploitation.

Rule 2: It Must Be Temporary

The final two months before an Ironman are brutal—they often involve injuries, exhaustion, and disappearing weekends. But post-race, you are on cloud nine, and then there is the recovery. The discomfort was temporary.

I learned this lesson from my work in advertising.

Early in my career at BBDO, a large advertising agency where I cut my teeth, the rhythm was guaranteed: one night a week past midnight. One night a month pulling an all-nighter. When deadlines stacked up or pitches overlapped, you'd hit back-to-back overnights that left you seeing double by morning. It hurt. But the work mattered. The quality and care showed in what we produced. The discomfort had purpose— we were building something that needed that level of intensity to be great.

That background shaped me. It probably broke something in me, too. I still struggle with people clocking in and clocking out as if work is a shift at a factory. Long days don't register as exceptional to me— they register as Tuesday. I have to work hard on my flexibility, on my "softer" side, and on remembering that not everyone grew up in agencies where sleeping under your desk was a badge of honor.

There's a difference between productive discomfort and permanent suffering.

After one of my team members pulled three fourteen-hour days on a major shoot—the kind of intensity where you live and breathe the project—I kept my mouth shut when I saw him racing out the door at noon, heading for a weekend getaway. My instinct? That's quitting early. My better judgment? He needed to recover on his own terms.

The discomfort was temporary. It had to be. Otherwise, it's not discomfort—it's just how we work. That's when people break.

Companies that treat discomfort as the default setting are not sustainable. They mistake suffering for commitment. They build cultures where the all-nighters never end, where the intensity never drops, and where recovery feels like weakness. People don't burn out because the work is hard—they burn out because it never stops being hard. There's no rhythm. No release. No recognition that the sprint needs to end so people can recover before the next one.

That BBDO intensity? It worked because it wasn't constant. One night past midnight, not seven. One all-nighter a month, not every week. The rest of the time, we left at reasonable hours. We recovered. We came back ready to do it again.

When discomfort becomes the default setting, it stops being productive. It just becomes the cost of showing up.

Rule 3: It Must Mean Something

I'll be honest about Amazon. The environment was intense—more intense than anything I have experienced before or since. To this day, I still second-guess certain decisions because of how that experience shaped me. While our team created amazing work and pioneered customer-first thinking that seemed impossible at the time, that level of intensity isn't for everyone. Especially people who lean more on their EQ—their emotional intelligence—than pure analytical horsepower.

We were building infrastructure for the future of commerce. We were solving problems at a scale nobody else was even attempting. When you created systems that could handle millions of transactions, you could see your work changing the way people lived their lives. The discomfort had a purpose. It connected to something bigger than quarterly earnings or stock price.

Compare that to companies where people grind eighty-hour weeks just to hit quarterly numbers that don't mean anything beyond hitting quarterly numbers, and the discomfort serves no purpose except maintaining the discomfort. Where people with high EQ—the ones who understand that engaged teams outperform burnt-out teams every time—get pushed out because the culture only values IQ and output.

The best people leave these environments because they can't answer the question, "Why does this matter?" without lying to themselves. They're not building anything meaningful. They're just suffering for the sake of suffering, burning out their emotional intelligence in service of someone else's spreadsheet.

As I've got older and led more teams, I've learned that you can build incredible things without destroying people's emotional capacity. The companies that last are the ones that balance analytical excellence with emotional intelligence—that understand when to push hard and when to recognize that your team needs to breathe.

That intensity at Amazon taught me what's possible when discomfort has meaning. However, it also taught me that not everyone needs to suffer the same way to create value. The real skill is knowing how to challenge people without breaking them, and how to create productive discomfort that builds capability rather than just endurance.

Rule 4: It Must Be Reciprocal

How you give back can be very different depending on the person. There are many things I like to give back that don't involve money or time off.

An art director on my team once delivered, and delivered, and then delivered more. After one particularly brutal period, I learned there was an international project in EMEA that needed someone with his specific eye. It meant a little extra work for him, but it also meant a trip to Dubai—a place he loves. When I asked him, his response was immediate: "Hell yes!"

That's the reciprocal part—understanding what makes each person tick. For this art director, the opportunity to work on an international project in a place that inspired him was worth more than a couple of thousand dollars of a bonus. Some people want recognition. Some want learning opportunities. Some want exposure to senior leadership.

The best leaders figure out what currency matters most to each person and pay them in that currency.

The companies that fail to observe this rule expect people to sacrifice without giving anything meaningful back beyond a paycheck. Then they wonder why nobody cares, why engagement scores crater, and why their best people leave for competitors who understand that reciprocity isn't just about compensation—it's about recognizing what each person values and making sure their investment pays dividends in that currency.

Businesses need to understand when to be uncomfortable and when to cruise. Athletes get this intuitively. The last two weeks before a race, you taper off. You don't do much work. But eight weeks before that? You're in hell.

I distinctly remember a training ride around, and then up Mount Rainier. We were peaking for a race, lean and strong. It was a non-typical hot, dry, windy day in the Pacific Northwest. The plan was roughly a hilly 140 miles—about seven hours at just under threshold pace. At about six hours, I completely ran out of steam. My body couldn't get enough calories in. I sat by the side of the road gathering my thoughts for what felt like ten minutes as I consumed calorie after calorie.

The plan became survival. If I dropped my heart rate, if I only put out a certain amount of watts and controlled the effort, I would get back to the car. It was a great learning experience for a race, because, just as in business, things will go wrong. It's guaranteed. We always trained for things to go wrong. Business is no different.

I ran the Phoenix Marathon many years ago—not a race I enjoy. In fact, it is a soul-sucking experience, but it had a purpose. A friend I was running with totally blew up, and we ended up running the rest of the race together. But all the time in my head, I was doing the math. I had to finish before approximately 3:15 PM to qualify for Boston. For the last five or six miles, I was constantly calculating—helping my friend across the finish line while making sure I also hit my time.

Making a plan as you go is sometimes the best way. You have a goal, things change, and things go wrong. However, if you pause and make a plan, it's the best way forward.

The Foundations of training and the belief system our coach built individually for us—that's what got us there. Training is about creating belief. And you create belief by going through hard things and coming out the other side. Those words of belief—they become Foundations.

Discomfort builds mental calluses. In 2002, I was trekking through Eastern Europe, living on $9 a night for cheap hostels and pizza. People on trains would tape their passports to their hands at night so they could sleep without being robbed. I'd book a hotel room every few weeks just to use the washing machine.

I trekked from Kashmir to Northern India in the late 90s by myself. The borders were safe then; you could trek in summer at high altitude without getting cold. I bought a bottle of water from a store, thinking it was from a bottling plant, filtered and everything. Then I was sitting by a stream, and there was a kid filling up reused bottles with a bottling cap thing, selling them right back to the store. I had to use iodine tablets and a hand pump after that, to protect against dysentery.

Growing up in Australia shaped this mindset for me. There's a saying there: "She'll be right." Get bitten by a jellyfish or a snake— she'll be right, we'll get over it. The attitude is very laconic. During World War I at Gallipoli, the British would send the Australians out of the trenches first because they knew we'd just get out and go. They were used as cannon fodder, then the British would follow after.

The harshness of the Australian environment, the isolation of growing up where we grew up—it's the same in some parts of the US, like Montana—it creates this relationship with discomfort. There's something about being alone and being comfortable by yourself, and putting yourself in situations where you have to learn to adapt, that's truly amazing.

Outside of marriage and my daughter, one of the best moments of my life was with my friend Peter in Sydney Harbor. We were sea kayaking through the Heads in a twenty-three-foot double kayak with container ships coming up behind us. We survived that, then got caught in a torrential thunderstorm. We couldn't see ten feet ahead. We were covered in salt, with the rain just pounding down, cleansing everything. Without a doubt, one of the best moments of my life. Peter and I don't talk often—maybe every couple of years—but that moment sticks in my mind as one of the most magical. It's never the five-star hotel rooms you remember. It's crossing a finish line with a friend, or getting caught in three feet of unexpected snow in the mountains and just waiting it out.

The discomfort is what stays with you. Ask anyone about the handful of best moments in their life—outside of marriage, kids, work promotions—and I guarantee most will be really simple. The uncomfortable, unexpected, unplanned moments that somehow become the stories you tell forever.

David Goggins calls it "callusing the mind"—building mental toughness through repeated exposure to discomfort. He doesn't look like a superhuman. He's just an average-looking guy who's developed an extraordinary capacity for discomfort through repetition. Research on Navy SEAL training confirms what Goggins learned first-hand: mental toughness isn't inherited, it's built.

Organizations can build these same calluses through deliberate practice. Amazon kept the "Day One" mentality even with 1.5 million employees—always building, always unsatisfied, always pushing. That's uncomfortable. Nevertheless, that discomfort is what kept them from becoming complacent.

Make teams small enough to feel the discomfort directly. Amazon isn't really one big company—it's thousands of small companies. Each leader owns their business, feels the pressure, and makes decisions that matter. This controlled discomfort builds organizational resilience over time.

You don't need to send people to Ironman training or Navy SEAL boot camp. But you do need to understand the rhythm.

Ask yourself: when was the last time we pushed hard? And when did we last give people real recovery time? Not fake recovery like "unlimited PTO (Paid Time Off)" that nobody takes. Real recovery where the pressure actually releases.

Ask whether people are opting into the hard projects, or we are forcing them. If your best people are avoiding the challenging work, it's because they don't see the point. The discomfort isn't meaningful or reciprocal.

Ask what calluses we are building. Are we getting better at handling discomfort, or are we getting more fragile? Every time you remove a challenge to make people comfortable, you're weakening the organization's immune system.

The goal isn't constant suffering. It's not toxic positivity either. It's understanding that growth comes from the rhythm—the push and the recovery, the discomfort and the reward, the challenge and the rest.

Companies that master this rhythm don't burn people out. They don't coddle them either. They build resilient teams that can handle whatever comes next. At the end of the day, being uncomfortable is a good thing. Being used to being uncomfortable is even better.

9
THE MEETING WITH JEFF

From my time at Amazon, some proof that thinking inside-out kills companies.

Just months into my tenure at Amazon, I was invited to my first meeting with Jeff Bezos. I thought I was ready.

With my leader, and other colleagues, we'd constructed what I believed was a bulletproof narrative argument discussing growing advertising revenue through brand dollars as opposed to retail dollars only. At that time, Amazon's advertising revenue included brand dollars, but it was relatively small compared to the search dollars. The document was black and white, double-sided, 10.5 Times New Roman, six pages plus an eye-watering appendix. This document was a mechanism called the Working Backwards document (or PRFAQ—press release and frequently asked questions). And every Amazon PRFAQ looked exactly like this—with no exceptions, no creativity, and no mercy.

From my advertising background, I knew the opportunity was there. We even had an off-site summit where the team flew in from around the globe to analyze the opportunity before this meeting: market size, competitive landscape, revenue projections, and implementation timeline. According to public data, Amazon's ad revenue was approximately $1 billion at the time. Today, it's somewhere between $46 and $50 billion. Amazon was sitting on a goldmine, and we hadn't even started digging.

I wore a collared shirt to the meeting, rather than my usual untucked T-shirt. I was nervous. Jeff was late. While secluded from standard conference rooms (Jeff had a private elevator for security reasons), this room was typical of its kind. It was in the Day One building, featuring a light grey table, light grey chairs, brushed cloth panel walls, and a large screen. In the middle of the table, looking lonely, was a container of red Bic pens.

When he walked in, the room changed. The air got quieter.

Like all Amazon meetings, we began by reading the document in silence. Red pens scribbling. Twenty-five minutes of absolute silence except for the scratch of pen on paper and the occasional grunt. Then thirty minutes. I suffocated in that silence.

Jeff pushed back from his chair. Backs stiffened.

"What I want you to do," he said, looking around, with his voice as flat as Kansas, "is walk away from this document. Come back in four to six months when you know and think more about Amazon and how we operate. And I want you to rewrite the document entirely from a customer's point of view, rather than Amazon's point of view. What we are going to deliver to the customer as opposed to what we're going to build and how we will make money."

Then he left.

Meeting over. Ego shattered.

I sat there stunned, trying to process what had just happened. Six weeks of work dismissed in seconds.

I hadn't even said a word. No one had said a word.

People looked at me with a mixture of sympathy and relief because most of the room had pre-read the document. The conference room felt smaller and hotter.

The analysis was solid. The numbers were correct. The opportunity was real. The rules were followed, every box checked, and every page formatted exactly to boring Amazon standards.

And that was the problem.

The document was written about Amazon, for Amazon, from Amazon's perspective. Six pages were spent explaining how we could make money without once genuinely considering what problem we were solving for customers and advertisers. We'd created an inside-out strategy in a company built on outside-in thinking.

The document discussed topics such as "leveraging our platform," "monetizing our traffic," and "capturing brand dollars." Corporate speak that meant everything to us and nothing to the millions who actually used our site and relied on our delivery. It was written like a consultant, not like someone who actually cared about customer experience.

Amazon's thought process completely inverted traditional business methods. Most companies start with what they have and figure out how to sell it. Amazon starts with what customers need and figures out how to build it.

Inside-out thinking is so natural that most companies don't even realize they're doing it. It starts with innocent questions:

- What are our capabilities?
- What are our assets?
- What's our competitive advantage?
- How can we monetize what we have?
- What does the stock market want?

These seem like smart business questions. They're not. They're narcissistic business questions. They assume the world cares about what you can do rather than what needs to be done.

I'd spent my entire career building from the inside out. Here's what we have, here's how we package it, here's how we sell it. The customer was an afterthought, a target, a wallet to be opened. I'd never genuinely started with their needs and worked backward.

At advertising agencies, you start with what the client wants to say, then figure out how to make people listen. The brief comes from the brand team: "We need to communicate our new formula," or "We want to own the concept of freshness," or "Our research shows we need to reach millennials." Then you craft messages, test them, refine them, and push them into the world.

The customer is never in the room. They're data points, demographics, and personas. "Urban millennials who value authenticity." "Suburban mothers concerned about health." "Digital natives with disposable income." Abstractions that make it easier to sell to them without actually thinking about them.

This inside-out disease infects every part of traditional business:

Product development starts with "What can our factory make?" instead of "What are our company's Foundations?"

Marketing starts with "What's our message?" instead of "What do customers need to hear?"

Sales starts with "How do we hit our targets?" instead of "How do we solve customer problems?"

Strategy starts with "How do we grow?" instead of "How do we serve?"

Not many start with the company's Foundations and our customer promise.

The following months after the PRFAQ meeting with Jeff were brutal. I had to unlearn twenty years of global advertising agency thinking.

I spent time with the retail teams, learning how they thought about customer experience. I interviewed sellers who were already spending money on other advertising platforms. I spent time with advertising agencies trying to spend money. I went to our distribution centers. I began to ask more: what worked? What didn't? What did they wish they could do on Amazon that they couldn't do anywhere else? Not from a capability standpoint, but from an outcome standpoint.

Instead of "we can offer targeted display ads," it became "sellers want to help customers discover products they didn't know they were looking for." Instead of "we can provide detailed analytics," it became "sellers want to understand which customers become long-term buyers, not just one-time purchasers."

Every insight began with a customer need, not Amazon's capability.

Five months later, I walked into a smaller conference room with a completely different document. The same format—six pages, Times New Roman, double-sided. Completely different thinking. This time, it was written from a customer-first point of view—how advertising on Amazon could improve a customer's life, make shopping more efficient, and help them discover products they didn't know they needed. Revenue wasn't the goal; it was the outcome. Customer obsession wasn't the outcome; it was the goal.

The document explained how advertising could enhance product discovery for customers, how it could help sellers connect with the right shoppers, and how it could make the whole ecosystem work better for everyone involved. I wore the same collared shirt. The reading period felt different this time. The silence was still total, but less suffocating. The meeting became a conversation about possibilities rather than a judgment on failure.

That document rewrite wasn't just about advertising. It was about understanding Amazon's entire operating philosophy.

When Amazon launched Prime, Wall Street thought they were insane. Paying for shipping upfront would destroy margins. But Amazon wasn't thinking inside-out ("How do we make shipping profitable?"). They were thinking outside-in ("Customers hate paying for shipping and waiting for packages").

When they created AWS, they weren't thinking, "How do we monetize our excess server capacity?" They were thinking, "Companies need computing power without massive capital investment." The fact that Amazon had already built this capability was secondary to the customer's need.

When they opened physical bookstores after "killing" physical bookstores, they weren't contradicting themselves. They were solving a different customer problem: the need to discover books through browsing, to touch and feel before buying, and to have immediate gratification for certain purchases.

Every major Amazon innovation follows the same pattern:

1. Identify a genuine customer frustration
2. Work backward to a solution
3. Figure out if it's technically possible
4. Determine if it can eventually be profitable
5. Build it even if steps 3 and 4 are uncertain

This is why Amazon could lose money for twenty years while building one of the most valuable companies in history. They were accumulating customer trust, not quarterly profits. They were solving real problems, not optimizing financial metrics.

My first document represented everything wrong with traditional business thinking. However, it wasn't unique to me—it was how I'd been trained, how I'd succeeded, how the entire business world operated.

That failed document had sections like:

- "Revenue Opportunity Analysis" (what we could make)
- "Competitive Landscape" (what others were doing)
- "Technical Capabilities" (what we could build)
- "Market Sizing" (how big the opportunity was)

Notice what's missing? Any genuine consideration of customer problems. Any deep thinking about user experience. Any evidence that customers actually wanted what we were proposing.

I'd treated customers as inputs to our model rather than the reason for our existence. I'd done exactly what every consultant, every MBA program, and almost every business book taught: analyze the market, identify the opportunity, and build the business case.

However, Jeff saw through it immediately. Not because he's a genius (though he might be), but because he'd trained himself to think differently. Every time someone presented an inside-out idea, he'd ask the same questions:

- "How does this help customers?"
- "What problem does this solve?"
- "Why would customers care?"

Simple questions. Devastating results for inside-out ideas.

During my change from inside-out to outside-in thinking, I learned the difference between inputs and outputs.

Most companies manage outputs:

- Did we hit our revenue target?
- Did we launch on time?
- Did we achieve our market share goals?

These are all outputs—the results of work already done. By the time you measure them, it's too late to change them. You can't manage outputs; you can only report them.

Amazon manages inputs:

- How many customer contacts did we have?
- How many experiments did we run?
- How many customer problems did we identify?

Inputs are controllable. You can decide to have more customer conversations. You can choose to run more experiments. You can deliberately seek out more problems to solve.

When you manage outputs, you're always looking backward. When you manage inputs, you're always looking forward. When you optimize outputs, you get better at what you're already doing. When you optimize inputs, you discover what you should be doing instead.

This input focus extends to everything:

- Instead of measuring customer satisfaction (output),
  measure response time to customer issues (input)
- Instead of measuring innovation (output), measure the
  number of experiments run (input)

- Instead of measuring quality (output), measure the number of defects caught before shipping (input)

Every company says they're customer-focused. It's in every mission statement, every investor presentation, and every CEO speech. But most companies can't actually make the shift from inside-out to outside-in thinking, and here's why:

The Quarterly Earnings Trap: Public companies have to report quarterly earnings. Wall Street punishes misses severely. This creates overwhelming pressure to think inside-out: "What can we do this quarter to hit our numbers?" Customer problems rarely align with quarterly deadlines. The same is true for salespeople, whom I admire. Hitting their numbers is their number one goal. However, at what detriment?

The Sunk Cost Prison: Most companies have massive investments in existing capabilities—factories, technologies, expertise, and relationships. Inside-out thinking maximizes these investments. Outside-in thinking might make them obsolete.

The Expertise Blindness: When you're great at something, you want to apply it everywhere. If you're a hammer, everything looks like a nail. If you're great at advertising, every problem looks like a messaging challenge.

The Data Delusion: Companies love data because it feels objective. However, most data is inside-out: our sales, our costs, our metrics. Customer needs are often qualitative, emotional, and hard to measure. So companies optimize what they can measure (their own operations) rather than what matters (customer problems).

After my failed first Amazon document, I developed a process for inverting from inside-out to outside-in. It comes down to five questions that should precede any major initiative.

Question 1: What specific frustration are we solving?

Not "What opportunity do we see?" but "Where are customers actually frustrated?" Frustration is energy. It's motivation. It's willingness to change behavior and pay for solutions.

CarMax understood this when they eliminated haggling from car buying. They didn't ask, "How can we sell more cars?" They asked,

"What do people hate most about buying cars?" The answer was obvious: the negotiation game. The uncertainty. The feeling of being manipulated. CarMax built their entire business around removing that single frustration.

If you can't name the specific pain point you're addressing, you're building from the inside out. Companies confuse opportunity with frustration, or market size with actual customer pain. They aren't the same.

Question 2: Can you write this proposal from the customer's perspective?

Not about them. As them. Use "I need..." instead of "Customers want..." This isn't semantic—it forces you to inhabit their viewpoint rather than project onto them.

When I rewrote my Amazon document, I literally started sentences with "I'm a seller who..." and "I'm a shopper who..." Every time I caught myself writing "Amazon will..." or "The platform can..." I stopped and reframed it from the customer's lived experience.

If you can't write your entire strategy document in the first person as your customer, you don't understand their perspective well enough to serve them.

Question 3: What's the perfect end experience, and what does it require?

Work backward from the ideal outcome. Don't start with your current capabilities and work forward to what you could build. Start with what should exist and work backward to what's required.

This is Amazon's "Working Backwards" process made into a question. Before they built Prime, they didn't ask "What can we do with our logistics network?" They asked, "What would perfect e-commerce feel like?" The answer: Free, fast shipping with no mental calculation about whether an order qualifies. Then they worked backward to figure out how to build it.

Most companies do this in reverse. They inventory their assets, then try to find applications. That's inside-out thinking. Outside-in thinking starts with the destination and figures out the path.

Question 4: Does this strengthen our Foundation, or just boost short-term numbers?

This is where discipline matters most. Will this initiative reinforce who you are and what you stand for? Or does it just look good on a quarterly earnings call?

If an idea requires you to compromise your Principles for short-term gain, kill it. If it only benefits your company without meaningfully improving the customer experience, kill it. "This will increase our margins" is not a customer benefit. "This will grow our market share" is not a customer benefit.

The hardest part of being Foundation-driven is saying no to profitable opportunities that don't align with the Foundation. However, every compromise weakens what makes you distinctive. Every deviation from your Principles makes the next deviation easier.

Question 5: How do we measure the customer outcome, not our revenue?

Instead of "This will generate $10M in revenue," ask "This will save customers 10 hours per month," or "This will reduce customer frustration by 40%" or "This will help customers accomplish X that they couldn't do before."

This is the difference between managing inputs and managing outputs. Revenue is an output—a consequence of customer value created. Customer time saved, problems solved, or capabilities unlocked are inputs—the things you can actually control and improve.

When you measure customer outcomes, the business outcomes follow. When you measure only business outcomes, you end up optimizing for the wrong things.

These five questions don't guarantee success. But they guarantee you're at least solving the right problem. They force you to start outside and work in, rather than starting inside and projecting out.

Most companies will read these questions, nod in agreement, and then immediately revert to inside-out thinking—because these questions are hard. They require you to admit you might not understand your customers as well as you think. They require you to kill ideas that could make money. They require patience when the market demands immediate results.

However, if you can answer all five honestly—if your initiative passes every filter—you've probably found something worth building. Something about which your customers will actually care. Something that might make them upset if it disappeared tomorrow.

Do this consistently, and the numbers take care of themselves. Not in the next quarter. Not always in the next year. But over time, customer trust compounds into the kind of growth that can't be replicated by competitors optimizing for quarterly earnings.

If Amazon Prime disappeared, millions would be furious. If Amazon Web Services disappeared, the internet would partially collapse. If Amazon's recommendation engine disappeared, shopping would become significantly harder.

But if most companies' "innovations" disappeared? Their "revolutionary" new formula? Their "game-changing" app update? Their "disruptive" business model? Customers wouldn't notice or care.

That's the difference between inside-out and outside-in. One creates things that customers tolerate. The other creates things customers can't live without.

My failed Amazon document would have created something nobody needed. The revised document helped build something that generates $50 billion annually—not because we optimized for revenue, but because we solved real problems for real people. The irony is perfect: by focusing on customer value instead of our own, we created more value for ourselves than we had ever imagined.

When Amazon paid for first-class shipping while charging standard rates, they lost money on every package. When they built AWS, they burned cash for years before it became profitable. When they launched Prime, Wall Street crucified them for destroying margins.

Every genuinely customer-obsessed decision feels financially insane in the short term. That's why most companies can't do it. They're optimizing for quarterly earnings, not decade-long customer relationships. They're managing to Wall Street's expectations, not customer needs.

The math is brutal and honest:

Outside-in thinking costs more upfront. It takes longer to show returns. It requires investment with uncertain payoff. It means saying no to profitable opportunities that don't solve real problems. It means your competitors will mock you for "leaving money on the table" while you're building customer trust that will compound for decades.

Inside-out thinking feels safe. It's immediately profitable. You're selling what you already have. The returns are quick and measurable. Your quarterly earnings look great. Your stock price stays stable. And then, slowly, customers find better options. Your growth stalls. Your margins are compressed. Your brand becomes forgettable.

You can start with what you have and try to convince customers they need it. Or you can start with what customers need and figure out how to build it. One path leads to comfortable decline as customers find better options. The other leads to growth that compounds as customer trust accumulates—but only after you've survived the initial pain of putting customers first when it hurts your numbers.

The inversion isn't easy. It requires abandoning everything you think you know about business. It means killing projects that could make money today but don't solve real problems. It means investing in things that might not make money for years, but that improve customer experience in meaningful ways. It means explaining to your board why you're sacrificing short-term profits for long-term relationships.

Once you make the shift—once you truly start with the customer and work backward—everything else becomes clear. Strategy becomes obvious. Priorities become undeniable. Decisions become simple.

Because when you're genuinely solving customer problems, customers solve your business problems. When you're truly outside-in, growth isn't something you chase. It's something that happens.

You just have to be willing to suffer first. To invest before you earn. To build trust before you extract value. To focus on inputs that matter rather than outputs that look good in quarterly reports.

Most companies won't do this. They can't. The pressure is too great. The timeline is too short. Courage is too rare.

That's why outside-in thinking isn't just a better strategy. It's a competitive moat. When your competitors are optimizing for this quarter, and you're optimizing for the next decade, you're playing a different game entirely. One they can't win because they can't afford to lose first.

10

TRANSCENDING MEDIOCRITY

Admitting your product is average can become your greatest strength.

Most products are mediocre. They're not bad; they're fine. And "fine" is the new fail. If your chocolate tastes like candle wax and your energy drink tastes like cough syrup, you have two choices: try to fix the product (which is expensive and usually fails) or transcend the product. I'm going to show you how companies like Hershey's, Cadbury, and Red Bull admit their product is just the vessel, then use their Foundation to sell something far more valuable: a moment, a feeling, or an identity that no competitor can copy.

Walk into any Kroger, Safeway, or Stop & Shop. You'll find 50,000 SKUs, arranged the same way, with the same brands, at nearly identical prices. They've all optimized themselves into the same store. Now walk into Trader Joe's. 4,000 SKUs—less than a tenth of the selection. No name brands. No sales. No coupons. No self-checkout. They're terrible at everything supermarkets are supposed to be good at. They generate twice the revenue per square foot.

Most companies make mediocre products. Not terrible products—those fail quickly and cleanly. Mediocre products that work fine, taste okay, and perform adequately. The kind of products that no one loves but no one hates enough to change.

Hershey's chocolate tastes like candle wax mixed with sour milk. This isn't just my opinion. It's chemistry. American chocolate contains butyric acid—a compound that gives vomit its distinctive smell. Milton Hershey added it by accident in the 1900s, when fresh milk wasn't available, using a process that partially soured the milk. Europeans find it revolting. Blindfolded taste tests consistently rank Hershey's below store brands.

However, Hershey's doesn't just sell chocolate. They are selling the twenty-second mental vacation you take at 3 PM when your brain is fried and you need to feel human again.

Think about what you're actually competing against. Someone reaches for a Hershey's bar at 3 PM. They're choosing between chocolate and scrolling Instagram for five minutes. Between chocolate and walking to the break room to gossip. Between chocolate and whatever else gives them twenty seconds where they don't have to think.

Better chocolate won't win that fight. Better delivery of that mental pause will.

It is interesting to watch people in Kohler showrooms imagining their bathrooms. They picture themselves in a different life. The version where they take long soaks instead of quick showers. Where mornings feel less rushed. Where home actually feels like a sanctuary, not just the place they crash at night.

Hershey's owns 3 PM when your brain is fried. Red Bull owns 2 AM when you need to push through. Starbucks owns that morning ritual before work starts. IKEA owns Saturday afternoon when you're feeling domestic and optimistic about assembling furniture.

One moment. Owned completely.

Dying companies try to own everything—premium customers, budget customers, health-conscious customers. Different products for different moments for different people. They become nothing anyone remembers.

Case Study: Cadbury

Their chocolate was equally mediocre—sweeter than Hershey's, but still a far cry from real chocolate. They could have optimized their recipes, upgraded their cocoa, and competed on product quality. Instead, they did something that seemed insane.

They made an ad with a gorilla playing drums to Phil Collins's "In the Air Tonight."

No chocolate. No product shots. No taste claims. Just a gorilla in a recording studio, feeling the music build, then absolutely destroying the drum solo while "In the Air Tonight" reached a crescendo. It was weird. It was expensive. It had absolutely nothing to do with chocolate.

It was also genius.

The ad said what Cadbury couldn't say directly: our chocolate isn't the point. The feeling is the point. That moment of pure, unexpected joy. That break from the rational world. That little bit of inspiration throughout your day.

Sales increased 9% in the period following the campaign. But more importantly, Cadbury's brand consideration scores jumped 20%. People weren't buying Cadbury because it was good chocolate. They were buying it because Cadbury understood that chocolate was just an excuse for a moment of joy.

The ad worked because it was honest about what Cadbury actually sold—not premium chocolate, but accessible pleasure. Not sophisticated taste, but simple happiness. And not the product, but the feeling the product enabled.

Case Study: Coca-Cola

Coca-Cola produces 2.2 billion servings daily of what is essentially sugar water with coloring. The Coca-Cola Company is worth over $300 billion.

This is a company that understands Explorer State at its core. When Coca-Cola was named Creative Brand of the Year at Cannes Lions 2024 —the first time in its 137-year history—it wasn't for improving the formula. It was for being one of the first major consumer brands to fully embrace AI and generative technology while staying true to their Foundation of "Real Magic."

In early 2023, Coca-Cola became the first company to partner with Bain & Company and OpenAI, making them early adopters of ChatGPT and DALL-E for marketing. But they didn't stop at adoption—they went deeper. They committed $1.1 billion over five years to Microsoft's cloud and AI capabilities. They created "Create Real Magic," an AI platform that generated over 120,000 unique user-created artworks. They produced an entirely AI-generated Christmas commercial. They launched Y3000 Zero Sugar, a flavor co-created by humans and AI.

The head of go-to-market at OpenAI called Coca-Cola's AI strategy "the most ambitious we have seen of any consumer products company." That's a recognition that, while other brands were cautiously observing AI, Coca-Cola was in full exploration mode.

Coca-Cola never changed what they are. The Foundation—Real Magic, optimism, small moments of happiness—stayed constant. The Principles guiding decisions remained intact. What changed were the Characteristics and the organizational state.

CEO James Quincey personally drives these AI partnerships. He doesn't delegate cultural relevance or technological exploration to a CMO.

One of the oldest, most established brands in the world—a company that sells sugar water—chose to enter Explorer State aggressively while protecting their Foundation. They didn't wait for proof. They didn't form a committee to study AI for eighteen months. They partnered with OpenAI when it was still "relatively unknown," according to industry observers.

Coca-Cola Creations—limited flavors like "Dreamworld" with AR experiences, and "pixel-flavored" Coke for gamers—weren't product innovations. They were cultural conversations using new technology to express an unchanging truth: Coca-Cola creates small moments of magic.

The New Coke disaster of 1985 taught them something. When they changed the formula—the Foundation—people revolted. However, when they change everything around the product while keeping that core consistent, people celebrate. The new flavor didn't work? Return to Classic. The AI experiment gets criticism? Refine and continue. But keep exploring.

Most companies that are Coca-Cola's age are in a permanent Static State, defending yesterday's successes. Coca-Cola proves that longevity doesn't require rigidity. You can have sold the same formula since 1886 and still pioneer generative AI. You can be deeply traditional and radically experimental—if you know what never changes.

Case Study: Red Bull

Red Bull tastes like liquid Sweet Tarts mixed with cough syrup. It's aggressively unpleasant. Most people trying it for the first time physically recoil. The product itself is so bad that it almost seems designed to fail.

Red Bull sells wings. The liquid is just the delivery system.

They spend over $2 billion annually—about 30% of revenue—not improving the taste but owning extreme sports, music festivals, and human achievement. They sent a man to the edge of space to jump out of a balloon. They own two Formula 1 teams. They run a media house that produces films about people doing impossible things.

When Felix Baumgartner stood at the edge of space in 2012, about to jump from 128,000 feet, eight million people watched live on YouTube. The Red Bull logo was visible for all nine minutes and three seconds of freefall. Not as an ad. As part of the story.

That's transcendence. Red Bull knows their product is just caffeine and sugar in a can that tastes terrible. But what it enables—pushing past limits, achieving the impossible, and having wings—that's worth $8 for 8.4 ounces of bad-tasting liquid.

Their market share in energy drinks is 40% globally, despite being the worst-tasting major option. Monster tastes better. Rockstar tastes better. Store brands taste better. But none of them owns human achievement. None of them gives you wings.

Successful transcendence works the same way every time: admit what you really are, then transcend it.

Red Bull admitted they're a terrible-tasting caffeine drink. IKEA admitted its furniture is disposable. Hershey's knows its chocolate is mediocre. Honesty creates freedom.

Then they kept the product consistent while changing everything else. Don't try to fix mediocre chocolate—embrace it and focus on what it enables. Don't improve the taste—improve what the taste represents. The product becomes the constant. The meaning becomes the variable.

This requires choosing one transcendence, not many. You can transcend from energy drink to human achievement. You can't transcend in five directions at once. Red Bull didn't become a beverage company, a media company, AND a lifestyle brand. They became the embodiment of pushing human limits—and the drink funds that mission.

Coca-Cola's immersive doesn't improve the product, but it improves what the product means. Red Bull's F1 teams don't make the drink taste better. They make choosing Red Bull mean choosing excellence.

That's the difference between improving your product and transcending your category. One makes you slightly better. The other makes you irreplaceable.

Case Study: Louis Vuitton

When I worked for a branch of LVMH, I went into the LV flagship store on the Champs-Élysées. They have a store behind the store—if you're wealthy or have the right job at the company, you get access to it.

I am a nosey person, so I asked what they do with excess stock. The answer was short and simple. They prefer to destroy excess stock rather than put it on sale. That's harsh. But it's also the Foundation of the LV business model. They've remained consistent for decades about quality and craftsmanship. That Foundation is built on a philosophy: we'll never go on sale. We'll never devalue what we've made.

Even now, with Pharrell as creative director of LV, they stick to that core of quality. They'd rather destroy product than dilute the brand (and this means sacrificing the short-term gain for long-term success).

They transcend the product category by making bags that hold their value forever because they control supply with religious discipline.

The exclusivity is the product. The bag is just proof that you could afford exclusivity.

Louis Vuitton presents a different model that seems to contradict everything else in this chapter. They insist their product is exceptional. They define the category. They claim perfection. But look closer. What Louis Vuitton actually sells has nothing to do with the quality of leather or craftsmanship. Hermès makes better bags. Local craftsmen create superior products for less. What Louis Vuitton sells is the price itself. The exclusivity. The signal that you can afford exclusivity.

When they destroy bags rather than discount them, they're protecting the core product, which is scarcity. When they refuse sales, they're manufacturing the only thing that matters: the perception that their products are too valuable ever to be discounted.

This isn't a counter-example. It's the same framework from a different angle. Louis Vuitton long ago transcended "bags" to become "status." They just never admitted it publicly because that admission would destroy the product. Their core is the maintenance of illusion. They're incredibly honest about what they are—to themselves. They just can't be honest with customers because honesty would destroy the value.

Red Bull is Austrian. IKEA is Swedish. Louis Vuitton is French. There's perhaps something about companies from outside the US, and its optimization mindset, that means they understand transcendence better. They're not watching quarterly earnings as closely. They're not as afraid of investments that can't be measured in 90 days.

Not every attempt at transcendence works. When advertising agencies start winning awards for work that didn't run, or when any work is made for the purpose of self-glorification as opposed to doing the right thing by the customer, that's transcending away from your Foundation instead of from it.

Starbucks is trying to get back to its Foundation right now. They expanded so far into grab-and-go efficiency that they lost the coffee shop vibe. Now they're trying to help people stay in stores longer, and get back to being the third place. Sometimes transcendence takes you so far from your Foundation that you have to transcend back.

If I had to move a company from competing on product to transcending category, I wouldn't try to change the whole company at once. That's what consulting firms do—they come in with their frameworks and try to transform everything. But their job is not to transform a company. Their job is to get the next billing. And the next billing. And the next billing.

Instead, I'd act like the Navy SEALs—work in small groups, but think really big. Send in a handful of people to solve one really big problem. If I had to turn the tide on Hershey's, I wouldn't go in and try to change the chocolate business or the candy business as a whole. I would go in and try to change one thing, and make that one thing really, really good.

Pick one product, one SKU, or one moment. Don't improve the chocolate—fully embrace what it actually is: a mental break, not a food product. Build everything around that truth for that one product. The packaging becomes about the pause, not the ingredients. The marketing becomes about 3 PM redemption, not taste. The distribution ensures it's everywhere when that moment hits.

When that one product succeeds, something beautiful happens in organizations. The team that pulled it off becomes living proof that change is possible. Not consultants with theories. Not executives with mandates. But Sarah from marketing and David from product—people who eat in the same cafeteria, who complain about the same meetings, and who fight the same internal battles. They did something everyone said was impossible, and suddenly, impossible doesn't seem so impossible anymore.

People love seeing their peers succeed. It's human nature. When someone at your level, someone you know isn't superhuman, breaks through and gets recognized, it creates a different kind of energy than top-down transformation ever could. Other teams start asking: how'd you get that past legal? How'd you convince finance? Can you walk us through what actually worked? The conversations happen in hallways and over coffee—in the real spaces where real work gets done.

The antibodies that usually kill innovation—the "we've never done it that way" crowd—can't argue with results from their own colleagues. When the metrics improve, when customers respond, or when the CEO mentions it in the all-hands, the resistance starts to crack. Teams that were skeptical start proposing their own experiments. The phrase "like what Sarah's team did" becomes currency. Success becomes contagious, but authentic contagion, not forced adoption.

This is how real transformation happens. Not through massive change management initiatives that everyone secretly resents. Change doesn't happen through massive, resented management initiatives or expensive, eye-rolling consulting frameworks, but through one team proving what's possible, then another team wanting that same recognition, that same success, and that same feeling of actually mattering. Before you know it, you've got five teams running experiments. Then ten. Then it's just how the company operates.

If you try to change it all at once, the way a typical consulting firm does, you're going to fail. It's guaranteed to fail. How many companies have truly changed because of a consulting firm? I'd love to see a case study.

Transcend from the inside out, starting small but thinking big. One product that proves the model. One team that shows it's possible. One moment that you own completely. Then you let human nature do the rest—because people will always follow authentic success from their peers before manufactured change from above.

Dying companies spend their last days pretending their product is good, still optimizing their messaging, still believing that marginal improvements in a mediocre product will somehow matter. Escape the middle by admitting what you really are: in most cases, our product is mediocre, but that's not what you're buying.

You're competing against anything that provides a 20-second mental break. Innovate emotional delivery systems, not cocoa percentages. Build your brand on honesty.

If your product disappeared tomorrow, what would customers actually miss?

Would they miss the chocolate, or the afternoon ritual? Would they miss the taste, or the wings? Would they miss the furniture, or the pride of building?

If the answer is the product itself, you're in trouble. Products can be copied, improved, or replaced. However, if the answer is what the product enables—the moment, the feeling, or the belonging—then you've transcended.

The bottom line matters. Revenue, profit—all of it matters. Red Bull still needs to sell cans. IKEA still needs to move furniture. Hershey's still needs chocolate sales.

However, there are very different ways to that bottom line.

You can optimize your way there—better ingredients, lower costs, or faster production. That works until someone optimizes better than you.

Or you can transcend your way there—admit what you really sell, build your Foundation around that truth, and sell it with complete conviction. Your chocolate might be waxy. Your energy drink might taste terrible. Your furniture might be made of particle board. But if you transcend the category by knowing the limitations of what you really sell and selling on your Foundations, your chance of business survival is higher.

Nobody really cares about your product. They care about what your product does for their day, their mood, and their identity. Companies endure by understanding what their (sometimes) mediocre products do for people—and then delivering that with unwavering conviction.

11

MOMENTS THAT MATTER

Creating experiences customers can't forget.

Emotional peaks beat consistent adequacy every time. Your technology is the same as your competitors. Your supply chain is the same. Your talent pool is the same. You differentiate through how you make people feel, not what you make.

I call these "Moments that Matter."

For CEOs who understand their role as chief brand architects, these moments become the primary canvas for expressing company beliefs. They're not marketing tactics. They're leadership opportunities. Every touchpoint becomes a chance to demonstrate what your organization actually stands for. Moments that Matter can be expensive, and they can be expensive—but not as expensive as going out of business.

My friend Tom—employee number five at Amazon, back when Jeff's desk was an old door removed from its hinges, and Amazon was still in the book-only stage—told me a story that perfectly captures what Moments that Matter look like in practice.

A customer ordered a coffee table book on Amazon.com. For someone ordering a coffee table book, presentation matters. These aren't just books; they're statements about who you are, what you value, what you want people to know about you when they walk into your living room. They sit on display, part furniture, part conversation starter, part identity.

When Amazon received the book from its supplier, it had a noticeable scratch across the front cover. It was not damaged enough to affect the reader, but enough to matter. If you want a beautiful coffee table book, the last thing you want is damage. You want perfection. You want something that makes you proud when guests notice it.

Jeff could have processed this as a standard return. Ship the damaged book, wait for the complaint, process the return, and send a replacement. That's what every other company would have done. That's what the operations manual would say. That's what would be efficient.

Instead, Jeff asked Tom to write a personal letter to the customer: "Dear Mr. or Mrs. Smith, please find enclosed the book you ordered. We noticed the book has a scratch on the front cover. Please accept our apologies. We've ordered a new one that will arrive within a week. When we receive it, we'll ship it directly to you. But please keep this existing book free of charge."

This was before sophisticated inventory management systems. Before one-click returns. Before Amazon Prime existed. Before customer obsession was a business school case study. This was Jeff, personally ensuring that a single customer's experience was perfect, even if it cost the company money.

Imagine being that customer. You order a book. It arrives with a scratch, and your heart sinks a little. Then you see a personal letter from the founder of this new internet company, apologizing for the scratch you haven't even complained about yet, promising a perfect replacement, and telling you to keep the damaged one.

In that moment, that person became a customer for life. They probably told everyone they knew about this experience. In 1997, when most people were still afraid to put their credit card information online, this story probably convinced dozens of others to try Amazon.

Amazon understood another crucial Moment That Mattered: they knew that speed mattered.

They charged everyone flat-rate shipping, which was supposed to take a week. Standard shipping. Nothing special. From the beginning, and for a long time, they actually shipped *everything* Priority Mail, which meant two-day delivery in most cases. They systematically under-promised and over-delivered. They surprised customers with faster delivery than expected, every single time. It was more expensive for the company, but it made the customer experience better.

Both decisions cost Amazon money in the short term. Sending two books instead of one. Paying for expedited shipping while charging for standard. These weren't efficient decisions based on optimization. They weren't what most consultants would have recommended. However, they created emotional connections that drove long-term loyalty.

Amazon's One-Click ordering innovation emerged from the same customer-first thinking. Early on, during a company retreat breakout session titled "friction-free ordering," someone asked a simple question: how do we make ordering easier for customers who've already bought from us? These customers had already entered their address, credit card, and shipping preferences. Why force them to re-enter everything for each purchase? The solution—remember those details and let existing customers order with a single click—wasn't about building fancy technology. It was about recognizing that customers had already trusted Amazon once and reducing the friction for them to trust Amazon again. That focus on existing customer experience, on removing unnecessary barriers for people who'd already chosen you, became one of retail's most significant innovations.

Case Study: Chewy

Chewy has perfected Moments that Matter with even more emotional intelligence than Amazon. They've built a $50 billion company by understanding that pets aren't just animals—they're family.

Chewy has a Subscribe and Save model for pet owners. You tell them how much food your dog needs each month, and it shows up automatically. Set it and forget it. Convenient. Predictable. Efficient.

But what happens when a pet dies?

The owner is grieving. They're not thinking about canceling

subscriptions. They're thinking about the empty collar on the counter, the quiet house, and the walks that won't happen anymore. They're mourning a family member.

Eventually, maybe weeks later, the next shipment arrives. Forty pounds of dog food for a dog that's gone. That's when reality hits. That's when you remember to call Chewy to cancel.

Chewy recognizes this trigger immediately. Their data shows the pattern: long-term subscriber, sudden cancellation, reason selected: "pet passed away." They could process this like any other cancellation. Send a confirmation email. Remove from the database. Move on.

Instead, they do something remarkable.

First, they tell you to keep any unopened food. Don't return it. Donate it to a local shelter in your pet's memory. Turn your grief into something positive. Help another animal in need.

Then, a few days later, something else arrives. A handwritten note expressing condolences for your specific pet—using their name, and acknowledging the loss. Sometimes flowers. Sometimes, a painted portrait of your pet, based on photos from your account. Sometimes, a donation to a shelter in your pet's name.

This is economically irrational. Most business schools would say it's wasteful. You're spending money on customers who just canceled. You're sending flowers to people who will never order again. You're paying employees to write personal notes instead of processing new orders.

Except it's genius.

Most pet owners will eventually get another pet. It might be months or years, but they'll open their hearts again. And when they do, where will they buy their pet food? From the company that sent a generic cancellation email, or from the company that sent flowers when their dog died?

More importantly, what will they tell their friends? Every pet owner knows other pet owners. Dog parks are social networks. Veterinary waiting rooms are conversation hubs. That story about Chewy sending flowers spreads like wildfire through communities of people who spend $75 billion annually on their pets.

Case Study: BMW

Auto dealerships have always understood one Moment that Matters: the test drive. They know the statistics. Once you're behind the wheel, your likelihood of buying increases by 300%. Once you smell that new car smell, feel the leather, and hear the engine, you're psychologically halfway to ownership.

BMW and Volvo have elevated this to an entirely new level. They invite customers to pick up their new cars directly from the factories in Sweden or Germany. Both companies call it European Delivery. You fly to Europe (often with discounted airfare arranged by the company), tour the factory where your specific car was built, meet the people who built it, then drive your new car through the European countryside before it's shipped home.

It costs a fortune. The logistics are insane. The companies have to maintain visitor centers, coordinate with customs, arrange shipping, provide insurance, and train factory workers to give tours. Any efficiency expert would have a heart attack looking at the numbers.

Instead of picking up your car in a suburban dealership parking lot, you're standing in Munich or Gothenburg. Instead of a sales guy in a bad tie, you're talking to the engineer who designed your engine. Instead of driving around the block, you're driving through the Alps.

You're not just buying a car. You're buying a story you'll tell for the rest of your life. Every time someone compliments your BMW, you don't just say thanks—you tell them about that time in Munich. You've created an evangelist, not just a customer.

BMW processes about 4,000 European deliveries annually. Each one creates a customer with 70% higher lifetime value than traditional buyers. They buy more BMWs. They maintain them better. All because BMW turned the moment of purchase into a pilgrimage.

Case Study: The Telcos

The telecommunications industry demonstrates what happens when companies create the opposite of Moments that Matter—when every interaction damages rather than builds the relationship.

These companies literally sell human connection. Every phone call carries emotion—tears of joy, words of comfort, declarations of love, or final goodbyes. They own the infrastructure of every meaningful conversation happening across impossible distances.

They should be celebrated. Instead, they're despised.

Comcast has become the company America loves to hate. Year after year, they rank dead last in customer satisfaction, below health insurance companies, below airlines, and even below the IRS. Their customer service calls have become internet memes. "Comcast Hell" has its own subreddit with 50,000 members sharing horror stories.

I don't belong to Comcast because I want to. I belong because I have to. You've created a hostage situation.

Every touchpoint with a telco is designed for their convenience, not yours. The automated phone system takes fifteen minutes to reach a human. The service windows span eight hours. The contracts are designed to trap rather than serve. The bills require a forensic accountant to explain them.

They've systematically eliminated every opportunity to create a positive emotional connection. When your internet goes down, and you need to work from home, they tell you someone might come between 8 AM and 6 PM next Tuesday. When you try to cancel, they transfer you six times. When you have a problem, they make you restart your modem seventeen times before admitting it's their infrastructure.

These companies forgot there's a human on the other end trying to call their mom, desperate to hear she's okay. They forgot that their product isn't bandwidth—it's belonging. They turned every moment into an anti-moment, every interaction into irritation.

When I was working on the Verizon account, we were mapping out the email journey for someone who had just bought a new phone. Within two months, customers were getting around fourteen emails from Verizon.

Fourteen.

You've just spent a lot of money on a brand new phone. You're excited. You want to enjoy it. But no. Three emails from the store. One from the service team. One from "your account." Different departments, different systems, and nobody talking to each other. Just bombardment.

I remember thinking: Just let people enjoy their phones.

This is the moment that should matter—you have a new device that's going to be part of your life for the next two years. It's going to hold your photos, your conversations, and your memories. And instead of celebrating that moment with you, instead of making you feel good about your purchase, we're treating you like a lead to be nurtured through marketing automation.

The irony is that telcos should own this moment better than anyone. They're literally enabling human connection. However, they've become so obsessed with internal metrics—open rates, click-throughs, and customer-lifetime-value calculations—that they forgot the customer just wants to make a call, or send a text, and feel connected.

When you optimize for your convenience instead of theirs, when you measure emails sent instead of relationships built, when you treat moments of joy as opportunities for cross-selling, you don't create customers. You create people who tolerate you until something better comes along.

Amazon taught me to measure the inputs, not the outputs. Most leaders only measure outputs—did we hit the revenue target? Did we launch on time? By the time the deadline hits and the work is done, there's no point in measuring. You can't change the past.

If you measure inputs, you can actually improve outcomes. Instead of tracking whether we hit our sales target, we tracked how many customer conversations our salespeople had. Instead of measuring launch dates, we measured how many experiments we ran. Instead of counting successes, we counted attempts.

Amazon was relentless on stats and data about these inputs. Not because they loved spreadsheets, but because inputs are the only thing you can actually control. You can't control whether customers buy. You can control how many customers you talk to. You can't control whether a product succeeds. You can control how quickly you iterate based on feedback.

This philosophy extends to Moments that Matter. Don't measure customer satisfaction scores (output). Measure how many personal notes your team writes (input). Don't measure retention rates (output). Measure how many surprise-and-delight moments you create (input).

These Moments that Matter can be expensive and inefficient—corporate donkey meat that companies have to choose to consume. Sending two books instead of one. Writing handwritten notes instead of automated emails. Flying customers to Europe instead of delivering to driveways.

Every spreadsheet says these are terrible decisions. Every consultant would recommend eliminating them. Every efficiency expert would have a heart attack.

Companies are often so focused on measuring inputs and outputs that they forget about the human moments in between. Those moments when a customer first touches your product, first experiences your service, or first realizes the value you've created for them. These aren't metrics. They're memories.

When it comes to creating a space inside your home, the moment that matters isn't when you buy a Kohler faucet online. Anyone can process a transaction. The Moment that Matters is the first time you turn on that faucet in your newly renovated kitchen and see the space transformed.

This connects to reality TV and home makeover shows, with their dramatic reveals. The gasps. The tears. The "Oh my God, is this really my house?" moments. That's what we're really selling. Not fixtures. Transformation.

When someone's renovating their kitchen, they're not just updating appliances. They're imagining dinner parties with friends, holiday meals with family, and morning coffee in a space that finally feels like them. I believe Kohler's job is to be part of that imagination, to help them see not just products but possibilities.

After studying hundreds of these moments across industries, a few patterns emerge.

First, identify the transformation point. Every customer journey has moments where emotion peaks—where anxiety, joy, fear, or excitement are highest. These are your opportunities. For Amazon, it was the moment of opening the box. For Chewy, it was the moment of loss. For BMW, it was the moment of purchase.

Second, over-deliver on emotion. Don't just meet the emotional need—exceed it dramatically. Amazon didn't just apologize for the damaged book; they sent a second one free. Chewy doesn't just acknowledge pet loss; they send flowers and paintings. BMW doesn't just deliver a car; they create a pilgrimage.

Third, make it story-worthy. Will the customer tell someone else about this? Nobody tells stories about adequate service. Nobody shares experiences that meet expectations. However, when you create something unexpected, generous, or deeply human, it becomes currency in social conversations.

Every touchpoint is an opportunity to strengthen or weaken the relationship with your brand. The brands that stick with you are the ones that obsess over those moments and build their entire experience around them. You don't do this because the spreadsheet says it's smart. You do it because you're dealing with human beings, not metrics. Customers forget the details. But they never forget the feeling you left them with. That's what sticks. And those feelings—created in carefully designed moments—become the stories that build brands, create loyalty, and generate the only kind of growth that matters: the kind that comes from customers who wouldn't dream of going anywhere else.

When our family renovated our kitchen in Wisconsin, our daughter Eleanor was part of the entire process. She watched the old kitchen get demolished—her height marks on the doorframe was gone. The breakfast nook where she did homework was destroyed. It was another disruption, another change she didn't ask for.

However, she also watched it being rebuilt. She helped choose tiles, spent hours with the Kohler catalog picking faucets, and learned words like "backsplash" and "undermount." She was seeing transformation in real-time—the idea that spaces can be reimagined, and that what exists doesn't have to be permanent.

The moment the contractor finished and we walked into the completed kitchen, Eleanor gasped because she recognized it as something she'd helped create. "We did this," she said. Not "you did this." "We."

That's a Moment that Matters from a personal standpoint. The transformation. The participation. She learned that destruction can lead to creation, that temporary discomfort leads to lasting improvement, and that you can be part of making things better even when you're young and powerless.

Case Study: The Magic Castle

There's a hotel in Hollywood that beats the Four Seasons in terms of customer reviews despite having no spa, no fine dining, and no marble lobbies. The Magic Castle Hotel—a converted 1950s apartment complex —consistently ranks among TripAdvisor's top hotels in Los Angeles.

They don't compete on luxury. They compete on moments.

A red phone sits by the pool. Pick it up, someone answers "Popsicle Hotline," and minutes later, someone delivers free popsicles on a silver tray, with white gloves. Board games and DVDs appear at your door within minutes of requesting them. Magicians perform at breakfast— actual card tricks while you eat your eggs. Laundry is free, including the detergent, delivered to your room. There's a snack menu available 24/7 with candy bars and sodas, all complimentary.

None of this should work. The rooms are basic. The building is ordinary. The location isn't prime Beverly Hills real estate. However, the Magic Castle understands something that Chip and Dan Heath documented in their book, *The Power of Moments*: human beings don't experience life as an average. We experience it as a series of peaks and valleys, and we remember the peaks.

The Heaths' research revealed that we judge experiences based on their best moment and how they ended, not their overall average— what psychologist Daniel Kahneman called the Peak-End Rule. A week at the Four Seasons with perfect but predictable service becomes a blur. One night at the Magic Castle with popsicles delivered on silver trays becomes a story you tell forever.

The difference between forgettable excellence and memorable magic comes down to four elements that create what the Heaths call "defining moments":

Elevation rises above the everyday. It's not just good service—it's service that breaks the script. The Magic Castle's white gloves carrying popsicles. Chewy's flowers when your dog dies. BMW flying you to Munich to pick up your car. These moments transcend the transactional.

Insight rewires understanding in an instant. When that Magic Castle employee appears with popsicles on a silver tray, your brain has to recalculate what kind of place this is. When Amazon delivers before they promised, you realize they under-promised on purpose. When Southwest flight attendants rap the safety instructions, you understand this isn't going to be like other airlines.

Pride captures us at our best. IKEA doesn't just sell furniture—they sell the pride of building something yourself. The Magic Castle doesn't just do your laundry—they make you feel like someone who deserves to have their laundry done for free. These moments make us feel like protagonists in a better story about ourselves.

Connection bonds us to something larger. When everyone at the Magic Castle breakfast laughs together at the magician's trick, when Chewy acknowledges your grief with flowers, or when the BMW engineer who built your engine shakes your hand in Munich—these moments create belonging that transcends commerce.

Nobody posts Instagram stories about predictably adequate service. Everyone posts about the Magic Castle's Popsicle Hotline. Nobody tells dinner party stories about Marriott's consistent check-in process. Everyone tells stories about BMW's European Delivery experience.

The Magic Castle doesn't need to advertise. Their guests create more authentic marketing than any ad agency could produce. Every popsicle delivered on a silver tray becomes a tweet, a TripAdvisor review, or a story told at dinner parties. The $15 cost of that moment generates hundreds of dollars in earned media.

The multiplication effect only works when the moment is genuinely surprising. If every hotel had a Popsicle Hotline, it would become expected, therefore invisible. If every pet company sent flowers, Chewy's gesture would lose its power.

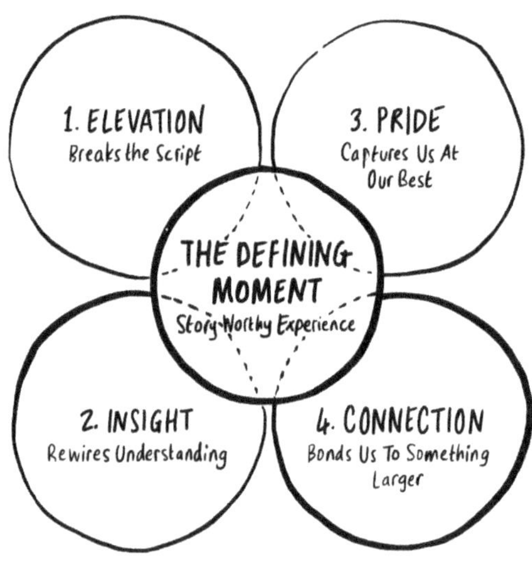

The Moments that Matter must be:

- Unexpected (breaking the category script)
- Specific (detailed enough to retell)
- Emotional (feeling, not just thinking)
- Shareable (simple enough to explain)

Finance will calculate the ROI and find it wanting. Operations will complain about complexity. Legal will worry about liability. HR will fret about fairness—why do some customers get flowers while others don't?

Every force in a traditional organization will push toward averaging out the peaks, smoothing the experience, and eliminating the surprises. This is why most companies end up with consistent mediocrity instead of memorable magic.

Protecting Moments that Matter requires leadership conviction that borders on irrationality. You have to believe that immeasurable delight beats measurable satisfaction. You have to defend concentrated investment against distributed improvement. And you have to choose stories over scores.

12

THE CEO IS THE NEW CMO

Leadership has become the ultimate brand differentiator.

For all intents and purposes, in our modern era, the CEO is the brand.

Richard Branson understood this before anyone had a term for it. When he wore a flight attendant's uniform—red skirt, full makeup, and heels—to serve drinks on a Virgin Atlantic flight, the business press called it a publicity stunt. They missed the point entirely. Branson was demonstrating something: he didn't just represent an extension of the Virgin brand. He *was* Virgin. Every stunt, every adventure, and every middle finger to convention reinforced what Virgin stood for: rebellious, fun, and human.

You can't hire an ad agency to create that. You can't delegate it to your CMO. You can't ask McKinsey's AI to generate it. It has to come from the person at the top, and it has to be genuine.

For decades, companies treated brand like a department. The CMO owned "brand strategy." The Creative Director owned "brand expression." Agencies created "brand campaigns." The CEO showed up quarterly to review.

This worked when competitive advantages lasted decades, and customers had fewer choices. That world is long gone.

~

Every Thursday at Apple, Steve Jobs held marketing and advertising reviews. Not quarterly. Not monthly. Weekly. These weren't approval sessions—they were teaching moments.

The meetings brought together key leaders who would pass the information down: product designers, creative directors, brand strategists, engineers, and media buyers. Jobs wasn't reviewing advertising. He was enforcing the core principles of the brand.

Every production value, every ad, every media buy, and every communication was a test: do we still know who we are? Are we solving real problems or just selling products?

The details were incredible and still live today. As a top-tier iconic company, they only showed up in the best places—only buying the top 1% of billboards and only in the best media placements. Rumor has it that there was one billboard in China they wanted, but the furniture and conditions around the billboard were subpar, so they rebuilt it.

The weekly meetings weren't efficient. Three-hour meetings to review work and discuss communications strategy, and media placements that could be approved via email aren't efficient. But it ensured that the content of the company matched the quality of the product. It enhanced the customer experience. Steve Jobs created philosophical density—when every decision, no matter how small, gets filtered through core beliefs.

The meetings compressed timelines. Teams didn't wait weeks for approvals. Jobs gave real-time input—sometimes harsh, always precise. Jobs cared about how Apple made people feel. Advertising wasn't about products—it was about values, identity, aspiration.

When Jobs personally reviewed every communication, he wasn't micromanaging. He was transmitting Apple's Core through the organization like an electrical current. Every person in those Thursday meetings left understanding not just what Apple did, but why it mattered.[1]

Case Study: Brian Chesky's Design Reviews

Brian Chesky at Airbnb doesn't just review marketing—he personally designs experiences. Not metaphorically. Literally. He sketches interfaces, writes copy, and obsesses over the smallest details of how a guest feels when they book their first stay.

Chesky calls himself the "Chief Design Officer" even though his title is CEO. He runs weekly design reviews where everything from app interfaces to host communications is scrutinized through one lens: does this create belonging?

When COVID hit in 2020, Airbnb's business collapsed. Bookings dropped over 80% in weeks. The company laid off 25% of staff, froze expansion plans, and shelved IPO ambitions. Cities were banning Airbnb. Hotels were lobbying against them. Travel had stopped.

Chesky didn't hire consultants to figure out positioning. He recognized something subtle: people still wanted to get away—just differently. Instead of global flights, they wanted safe escapes within driving distance. Private homes. Flexible stays.

Airbnb leaned into "near-not-far" travel. Extended stays surged. Entire homes outside cities dominated searches. The platform quickly adjusted its algorithms, filters, and marketing around this shift. Average stay length rose nearly 50%. Rural bookings more than doubled.

Airbnb had a pandemic tailwind, and they rode it hard because Chesky personally embodied the brand. Every decision became brand communication. Every feature became a belief statement. Every interaction reinforced belonging.

This isn't scalable by traditional metrics. CEOs aren't supposed to

---

1. Side note: Jobs didn't just believe in quality over quantity—he proved it. The clearest example was the 1984 television commercial that aired only once—during the Super Bowl, in, of course, 1984. Well, it did run one other time, December 1983, on a small San Francisco TV network to qualify for advertising awards.

spend time picking colors and editing copy. But when the CEO lives the Foundation, the company can pivot without losing itself.

The result? Airbnb went public in December 2020—one of the most successful tech IPOs of the decade—and hit a $75 billion valuation in 2021. This was not through financial engineering or cost-cutting, but through Chesky's obsession with making every touchpoint reflect the belief that everyone should belong anywhere.

The pandemic didn't save Airbnb. The Foundation did. The tailwind just revealed it.

Case Study: Howard Schultz's Store Visits

My former colleague Samie ran marketing at Starbucks for fourteen years. I once asked her about the rumor that described Howard Schultz visiting twenty to twenty-five stores every week. Not corporate visits with advance teams. Random walk-ins. He'd order a drink, sit in the corner, and watch. For him, this is where the rubber meets the road; this is where customers exist. And he believed in keeping a close connection to them.

While the number of stores visited weekly might not quite have been the high, Samie confirmed the rumor. The most important revenue period for Starbucks is Thanksgiving through Christmas— special cups, seasonal drinks, the whole holiday experience. They tracked sales data in real-time: morning numbers, afternoon numbers, evening numbers, cups sold, and coffee sold—if numbers were down, offers would come out.

Howard was deeply involved in almost every customer experience. This included the holiday cup design. One year, they changed from red to green based on research. Howard called from a store before the sun rose. The cups were wrong. Not because they were ugly, but because they broke the ritual. Red was Christmas at Starbucks. Red was warmth. Red was what customers expected.

Millions of dollars' worth of cups evaporated from stores, and millions more were made. The logistics team was furious. Finance had a meltdown. But Howard understood the customer: that red cup wasn't packaging. It was a promise.

Even today, when I'm with Samie at Starbucks, she straightens things on the condiment bar, and cleans up spills. It's built into her DNA that the experience *is* the brand, and that experience happens when people walk through the door.

The brand doesn't live in the headquarters and boardrooms. It lives in ten thousand moments happening simultaneously in ten thousand stores. The only way to maintain consistency at that scale is through a leader who is so involved and obsessed with the experience that everyone starts seeing it through their eyes.

Case Study: Ed Bastian's Operational Excellence

Ed Bastian at Delta understands something most airline CEOs don't: in a commodity business, the CEO's personal commitment to brand values is the only differentiator.

Every airline flies the same planes. They use the same fuel, follow the same regulations, pull into similar airports, and get food from the same kitchens. When everything is identical at 37,000 feet, the only difference is how they make you feel.

Bastian knows what business he's actually in. Delta isn't in the airline business. They're not even in the travel business. From their Foundation, Delta is in the service business. They know that people— their teams—are the inputs to the output, which happens to be flights.

Once you understand that distinction, everything Bastian does makes sense.

He doesn't delegate service to marketing. He personally flies Delta constantly—not in a corporate jet, but on regular flights, seeing what customers experience. When Delta's IT system crashed in 2016, stranding hundreds of thousands of passengers, Bastian didn't send out a corporate statement. He personally appeared in airports, talking to stranded passengers, and sleeping in the terminal with his team until the crisis was resolved.

This was a CEO living his Foundation: if you're in the service business, the CEO must be obsessed with the people delivering that service and the people receiving it.

Every operational choice—from buying new planes to training gate agents—is filtered through one question: does this demonstrate that we value our customers' time and comfort? More importantly, does it equip our people to deliver exceptional service?

This isn't a marketing message. It's an operational philosophy that starts with the CEO and cascades through 90,000 employees. When your Foundation is service, and you recognize that your people are your primary input, you invest differently. You train differently. And you lead differently.

The numbers prove it works. Delta's net promoter score is 44, compared to United's 10 and American's 3. Their operational reliability consistently ranks the highest among U.S. carriers. Their stock outperformed competitors by three time over the past decade.

However, the real proof is in how Bastian spends his time. While other airline CEOs focus on fleet optimization and route planning, Bastian focuses on the people who make service happen. That clarity about Foundation—knowing you're in the service business, not the airline business—is what lets a CEO turn operational excellence into brand loyalty. When you understand what business you're truly in, every decision becomes clearer. When your people understand it too, they don't just follow procedures. They deliver service.

Case Study: Elon Musk

Elon Musk demonstrates what happens when CEO brand leadership goes catastrophically wrong.

When Musk acquired Twitter in October 2022 for $44 billion, he inherited one of the most valuable brand assets in modern business. The Twitter bird was globally recognized. The word "tweet" had entered the dictionary. Within a year, he destroyed it.

The rebrand to "X" wasn't just a name change—it was brand vandalism at an unprecedented scale. But the real damage came from Musk himself becoming the brand. His political posts, his public feuds, and his management decisions—they all became inseparable from the platform.

Disney, Apple, IBM, and hundreds of others pulled billions in ad spend—not because the platform's functionality changed, but because they couldn't separate their brands from Musk's behavior. Brand safety matters. Where your brand shows up, and what it appears next to—these aren't minor details. They're existential questions.

Unlike Amazon and Walmart's ad platforms, which are embedded in commerce ecosystems, platforms like Twitter and Meta survive on advertising dollars alone. When brand reputation is at stake, CMOs pull spend. It doesn't matter how good your media sales team is. Musk hired one of the best media salespeople in the business as CEO — someone known as a tough, articulate negotiator who speaks both "brand" and "engineering." It didn't matter. You can't negotiate away toxicity.

The contamination spread to Tesla. The company had built its Foundation on progressive environmental values and found its early adopters primarily among Democrats up and down the West Coast. After Musk's Twitter acquisition, Tesla's brand favorability among Democrats dropped from 39% to 16%. Losing half your customer base because of a CEO's tweets isn't a PR problem—it's corporate suicide.

When you make yourself the brand, everything you do becomes brand communication. Every tweet. Every appearance. Every political position. You can't separate personal from professional. You can't say, "I'm speaking as Elon, not as Tesla's CEO." Customers don't make that distinction.

The Twitter-to-X debacle shows the ultimate risk of CEO-as-brand: when the CEO becomes erratic, the brand becomes erratic. When the CEO alienates audiences, the brand loses customers. When the CEO's personal agenda overtakes business strategy, billions in value evaporate.

Musk violated the first rule of Foundation Theory: he changed what never should have been changed. Twitter's Foundation was open discourse and real-time information. Instead of protecting that Foundation while evolving everything else, he torched the brand, alienated the user base, and destroyed advertiser confidence—all while believing his personal brand was strong enough to override decades of carefully built equity.

It wasn't.

~

Jeff Bezos was particular about who spoke publicly for Amazon. If you were to speak on stage or at an event, you would go through months of PR training. Not an hour—weeks. They'd teach you to pivot back to your specific talking points. How to talk, how to sit, and how to directly answer questions without saying anything. The aim was to protect the company and the brand. During mock training presentations in front of a dozen or so people, just as you're walking off stage thinking you're done, someone calls out: "Mr. Reeves, just one more question." It's designed to catch you off guard, to test whether you can maintain discipline when you think you're safe.

Jeff believed one bad incident could ruin everything, no matter how much good you do. That's why Amazon was so careful about who could speak publicly. But Jeff himself? He was always on brand because he WAS the brand. His laugh, his intensity, his letters to shareholders, and even the emails with just a simple "?"—everything reinforced Amazon's Foundations.

This discipline extends to every leader who truly embodies their company and brand. They're never off duty. Every interaction, every decision, and every public moment is brand communication.

Involvement doesn't mean domination. The best leaders understand when to step back, when to listen, and when to speak.

I remember being in Slovenia for a long shoot. The crew had built this stunning stairwell down a canyon into the ocean. It was brutally hot, with not a breath of wind. The building and crew had done phenomenal and fast work. On any shoot, you have craft services—food for the crew. We broke for lunch, and I deliberately went last, as I always do.

Someone noticed and asked, "You don't eat?" I said, "I eat, but I like to eat last. I want to make sure the crew gets fed. There are 70 of them, and I'm just sitting behind a monitor, and sometimes with AC and fans."

The most senior person in a room should go last. I'm not a fan of sitting at the head of the table situation. Leaders should stand behind their teams instead of in front of them.

This applies to creative sessions too. As an introverted person, I don't much like talking. I like talking last though. When you speak first as a leader, you set the tone, you influence the room, and you accidentally kill ideas before they're born. When you speak last, you hear what people really think. You get the unfiltered truth. You learn what your team actually believes, as opposed to what they think you want to hear. And importantly, the smartest person in the room is often the quietest person. I want to hear what they say. If I talk, they won't talk.

Companies are now creating six-figure roles called "Head of CEO Content"—entire positions dedicated to managing executive social media presence. Major corporations from PayPal to the largest hedge funds are hiring for these roles because the data is undeniable: 77% of buyers are more likely to purchase from companies whose executives are active on social media.[2]

This isn't a trend. It's the market sorting out who means what they say.

The mistake companies make is thinking they can outsource this. They hire teams to craft executive voices, ghostwrite LinkedIn posts, and manage the CEO's personal brand. They're missing the point entirely.

Jobs didn't need a content team because every word came from a genuine obsession. You could feel it. Schultz didn't need ghostwriters because he actually visited those stores, actually cared about that red cup, and actually lived the brand. The conviction was real, so the communication was real.

Now, more than ever, with AI and the Convergence Cascade, your competitors can copy your product. They can steal your people. They can match your prices. They can follow the same processes and technology. But they can't fake conviction. They can't replicate the consistency that comes from personal involvement. They can't manufacture authenticity when the belief isn't there.

When Brian Chesky talks about belonging, you believe it because he lives it. When Howard Schultz talks about the third place, you feel

---

2. 71% of consumers are more likely to buy from a company if its CEO is active on social media (Edelman, 2024) - Source: DSMN8 citing Edelman research

it because he's felt it in thousands of stores. When Jobs talked about the intersection of technology and liberal arts, every decision proved it.

The companies that fail? They are the one where the CEO treats the brand as a marketing function to be delegated. Leadership focuses on operations while "marketing handles the brand stuff." The person at the top can't articulate why the company exists beyond making money.

You can't outsource conviction. You either have it, or you don't. And if you don't, people can tell.

13

THE FLYWHEEL 2.0

Building momentum that compounds over decades.

Jim Collins gave us the framework for how momentum builds. Now, I'm going to show you the critical piece that was missing from the original diagram—the single gravitational force that makes the wheel actually spin in the right direction: the center. This is my practical update: the Flywheel 2.0. I'm going to show you what to put at the center, and how your Principles become the braking system that keeps the momentum from destroying you.

The story goes that the Amazon Flywheel was sketched on the back of a napkin at a coffee shop, late at night, by Jim Collins and Jeff Bezos in 2001. This was around the time of the dot-com crash, when everyone thought Amazon was finished. The stock had dropped from $107 to $7. Analysts were literally taking bets on when, not if, Amazon would declare bankruptcy.

However, Jeff and Jim weren't planning a funeral. They were building a framework for decades of compounding growth.

That napkin sketch would become one of the most studied business models in the world. Jim Collins deserves enormous credit for creating the flywheel concept—it's a brilliant framework that's helped thousands of companies visualize how their businesses create momentum. His work in *Good to Great* revolutionized the way we think about business transformation. The idea that companies can build self-reinforcing cycles where each element drives the next was genuinely groundbreaking.

Good to Great is one of the most important business reads out there. However, after working with the flywheel at Amazon for years and implementing it at multiple companies since, I've discovered something that builds on Collins's wheel. Not a correction—Collins was right about everything he wrote. But here is an evolution based on what I've learned by applying his framework in the trenches.

Collins showed us how momentum builds—push the heavy wheel consistently in one direction, and eventually, a breakthrough happens. Each turn builds on the previous one. No single action creates the transformation. It's cumulative.

What he didn't specify was what you're building momentum *toward*.

In Collins's original flywheel, there's nothing in the center. It's a beautiful circle of reinforcing activities, but no single gravitational force pulling everything together.

Jeff saw this gap immediately. He placed one specific thing in the center of Amazon's flywheel: **Growth**.

Not customer obsession—that's Amazon's Foundation, their unchanging truth about why they exist. Growth is the mechanism that makes the Foundation scalable.

Lower prices drive more customers. More customers drive higher volume. Higher volume drives better supplier negotiations. Better negotiations drive lower costs. Lower costs enable lower prices. The wheel spins faster with each rotation, all orbiting around Growth as the central force.

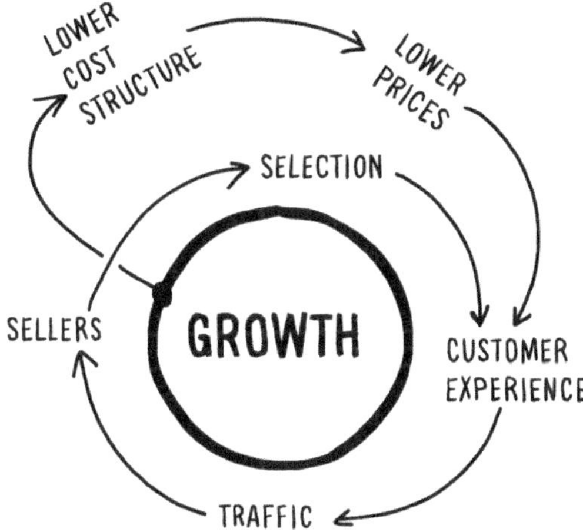

This is where Foundation Theory connects to the flywheel. Your Foundation never changes—it's your unchanging truth about why you exist. Your flywheel is the tactical system that serves the Foundation. The center of your flywheel should be the primary driver that enables your Foundation to scale.

For Apple, the Foundation is technology that feels human. The center of their flywheel is the intersection of technology and liberal arts. That specific focus drives every product decision, every design choice, and every experience they create.

For Tesla, the Foundation is sustainable transport. The center of their flywheel is vertical integration—batteries, charging infrastructure, software, and manufacturing. That's what makes the Foundation scalable at the speed required to matter.

For Airbnb, the Foundation is a sense of belonging. The center of their flywheel is trust—verified hosts, reviews, secure payments, and instant booking. Trust enables belonging at scale.

One specific thing in the center. Not your Foundation—your Foundation is what it serves. Not multiple priorities—Growth OR Trust OR Integration. One driver that makes everything else compound.

The thing about a flywheel is that it creates momentum through accumulated small wins, not individual big ones.

People try to solve everything at once. They want the transformation to happen in one quarter, one initiative, or one reorganization. They push with massive force once and wonder why the wheel doesn't spin faster.

Physics doesn't work that way. A flywheel responds to consistent pressure in one direction over time. Amazon didn't become Amazon overnight. They lowered prices slightly. Got a few more customers. Negotiated slightly better terms. Lowered costs incrementally. Then, they repeated the cycle thousands of times over twenty-five years.

Each rotation made the next one easier. Each small win created conditions for slightly bigger wins. But they were solving for the next turn of the wheel, not trying to spin it to maximum velocity in a single push.

Most companies abandon their flywheels because they don't see dramatic results immediately. They push for a quarter or a year, don't see exponential growth, and pivot to a different strategy. They never build enough rotations to reach the breakthrough point where momentum becomes self-sustaining.

Amazon's flywheel has been reinforced every single day for twenty-five years. The same wheel. The same center. The same reinforcing loops. That consistency—that refusal to chase shiny objects or pivot away when results feel slow—is what created unstoppable momentum.

How many companies can say that for fifteen or twenty years, their core strategy remained relatively unchanged? That they just added onto it, refined it, and reinforced it, but never abandoned it?

Consistency wins in the long run. As I have said, you need to sacrifice short-term revenue for long-term compound growth.

~

Every flywheel eventually hits a breaking point. There comes a time when the same speed that made you successful becomes the force that threatens to tear you apart. This isn't a flaw in the flywheel concept—it's physics.

Collins showed us how to build momentum. Experience taught me that momentum without governance eventually becomes destructive.

Amazon knows this intimately. They've hit breaking points multiple times.

Amazon Restaurants had perfect flywheel logic: more restaurants → more selection → more customers → more restaurants. But the wheel was spinning them away from their core Foundation. Delivery logistics weren't where Amazon could create unique customer value. They shut it down in 2019 after four years, not because it failed but because it was spinning too fast in the wrong direction.

The Fire Phone followed the flywheel perfectly: control more customer touchpoints → gather more data → serve customers better → expand the ecosystem. They killed it after one year; it was a $170 million write-off. The momentum had carried them past customer relevance into territory where they had no right to win.

This isn't failure—it's learning. It's what Principles are for.

This is how Principles control the flywheel. They're the braking system that stops momentum from becoming destructive. When the wheel starts spinning you away from your Foundation, Principles force you to slow down, break off pieces, and rebuild.

Amazon's Leadership Principles have been around for decades. They don't truly change—they're just reinforced through every decision, every meeting, and every hire. "Customer Obsession" stopped the Fire Phone. "Think Big, but Disagree and Commit" enables them to launch bold experiments. "Are Right, A Lot" helps them know when to kill initiatives that aren't working.

The Principles stop the out-of-control bus on most occasions. They're the governor on the engine that prevents your flywheel from spinning itself apart.

Here's how to build a flywheel that works:

1. Define your center with painful specificity—and never change it

Put one thing in the middle. Not "customer satisfaction" but "reducing delivery time to under one hour." Not "innovation" but "replacing human drivers with autonomous vehicles." The center must be so specific that it makes decisions obvious.

Then commit to it for decades. Your competitors will change strategies five times while you're refining your first flywheel. That's their weakness, not yours. Pick the right center and refuse to abandon it when it gets hard.

2. Map your reinforcing loops with brutal honesty

Identify how each element actually drives the next. Lower prices → more customers → higher volume → better supplier terms → lower costs → lower prices. Each connection should be causal and specific, not wishful.

Test every connection: does this actually cause that? Or are we just hoping it will? Most flywheels fail because companies draw arrows between things that don't actually reinforce each other. They want customer satisfaction to drive innovation to drive growth to drive satisfaction, but none of those connections hold under pressure.

If you can't explain exactly how element A creates element B, you don't have a flywheel. You have a wishlist.

3. Hire specialists who embody your Foundation—not generalists who fit anywhere

Jim Collins taught us to get the right people on the bus, and then put them in the right seats. But most companies miss his point. They hire for cultural fit first, then figure out where to put people. They end up with a bus full of smart generalists who can kinda-sorta do multiple jobs.

That doesn't work for flywheels.

You need people who are excellent at their specific function, and who also share your Foundation. Not "smart people who can learn anything" but "the best supply chain operator in the industry who believes what we believe."

When your flywheel is spinning fast, you can't afford learning curves. You need someone who executes their element flawlessly from day one while making decisions aligned with your Principles. Amazon didn't hire talented people and figure out what they should do. Bezos hired the best software engineers, the best logistics specialists, and the best merchandisers—people who were already world-class at their function and who embodied customer obsession.

The cultural fit ensures they make decisions consistent with your Foundation. The functional excellence ensures they can actually execute their part of the wheel. You can train someone to use your tools and learn your systems. You cannot teach someone to think like a world-class operator or instill genuine belief in your Foundation if they don't share those values.

4. Give single-threaded ownership with complete authority

Each element of your flywheel needs one owner. No committees, no dotted lines, and no shared accountability. One person who wakes up thinking about their element and has the authority to make it work.

Speed only happens when someone actually owns a decision—and has the authority to make it without begging for sign-off. If you don't trust them enough to act, you didn't hire the right person. A lot of companies pretend to give people ownership. Then they make them ask for permission for every move. That isn't ownership. It's a puppet show.

If you trust someone enough to own an element of your flywheel, trust them enough to make decisions about it. If you don't trust them that much, you hired the wrong person.

5. Build Principles that govern the wheel

Your Principles determine when to accelerate, when to maintain, and when to deliberately brake. Without them, momentum becomes dangerous. You'll keep spinning faster even when you're heading toward a cliff.

Amazon's Principles told them to kill the Fire Phone despite the momentum behind it. Your Principles should tell you when speed is carrying you away from your Foundation—and give you permission to slow down before you crash.

The flywheel is there to serve your Foundation. If it starts running the show, you've lost the plot.

6. Measure momentum, not just speed

Track how fast your flywheel spins and how efficiently it converts energy into results. Revenue growth without customer satisfaction isn't momentum—it's a wheel about to break.

The best test: are rotations getting easier? If the fifth turn is just as hard as the first, you don't have a flywheel. You just have work that never compounds. Real momentum means each turn requires less effort while producing more results.

If it's not getting easier, something in your wheel is broken. Find it and fix it before you spin faster.

Companies try to cram five priorities into the center of their flywheel. When everything is the center, nothing is. A flywheel with five centers doesn't spin—it wobbles until it breaks.

You need one thing in the center. For Amazon, it's Growth—not because they don't care about profit or people, but because Growth is what enables customer obsession at the scale required to matter.

Then companies make the specialist mistake. They hire smart people and assume they'll figure out their roles. But flywheels spinning at high speed need specialists who can execute their part flawlessly from day one, while also sharing the values that make the organization cohere.

Moreover, nobody plans for the point when momentum becomes dangerous. They assume speed always equals success. But Amazon Restaurants had perfect logic. Fire Phone followed the model exactly. The flywheel was spinning—it was just spinning them away from their Foundation.

You know your flywheel is working when decisions become obvious, each success makes the next one easier, and competitors can see what you're doing but can't replicate it because they don't understand what's really in your center.

You know it's breaking when momentum becomes the strategy itself, you're spinning faster but not sure why, and the thing that made you successful is now preventing future success.

The flywheel is a mechanism, like Amazon's Working Backwards document. It's a system that makes your Foundation operational. But it serves your Foundation—it doesn't replace it.

Put the wrong thing in the center, hire generalists instead of specialists, ignore the breaking points, or fail to maintain it for decades, and you'll build momentum that destroys rather than compounds.

Build it right, with your Foundation guiding it and your Principles governing it, and you create the rarest thing in business: compounding momentum that lasts for decades.

14

BUILDING ORGANIZATIONAL STRUCTURE TO FUEL GROWTH

Design organizations that make slow impossible.

"The new Ford F-150 is not good for mankind."

The insight was brilliant and uncomfortable. The new Ford F-150 was so superior to other trucks that it made competing brand owners feel inadequate. At the time, I was at JWT (WPP), an advertising agency whose primary client was The Ford Motor Company. With the new F-150, we weren't just selling capability; we were weaponizing insecurity. The campaign would acknowledge this directly—TV spots showing Chevy Silverado owners hiding their trucks at job sites, kids wanting their dads to drop them off around the corner from schools so they weren't seen in a Dodge Ram, dealership testimonials about Toyota Tundra owners trading in after seeing the F-150. And to top it off, we had psychologists discussing male insecurity issues that came with an inferior product.

It was provocative, memorable, and would have cut through the endless sameness of truck advertising where every brand claims to be "toughest" and "most capable," saying "it has a Hemi."[1]

---

1. "Hemi" stands for hemispherical combustion chamber—an engine design where the

We took the idea of "The new Ford F-150 is not good for mankind" to my boss. They were uneasy about it, but liked it, yet needed her boss's approval. Who needed his boss's approval. Who needed the global chief creative officer's approval. Each level took a minimum of three weeks. First, my boss spent a week "refining" the presentation. Then his boss needed another week to add "strategic context." Then the regional head wanted to "pressure test" it with internal focus groups.

Four months. Four months for an idea to climb the approval ladder, getting poked, prodded, diluted, and focus-grouped into submission. Into vanilla.

Here's how it worked: each person who touched the campaign had to justify their existence. By having an opinion. By adding "value." By making it "better." The psychologist angle? "Too edgy." The competitor comparisons? "Too aggressive." The insecurity insight? "Too negative."

By the time our idea came back down the chain, it had been transformed into another generic truck ad—indistinguishable from the last decade of truck ads. The bold concept that would have cut through the noise became just more noise.

Think about what we sacrificed for those four months of meetings. We could have tested the original campaign in market in two weeks. We could have created twenty other ideas in that time. We could have learned what actually worked instead of what people thought might work in a conference room. We could have been running the campaign while our competitors were still in their first approval meeting.

Ford was selling roughly 900,000 F-Series trucks per year during this period—more than one-third of the company's total U.S. vehicle sales. Tens of billions of dollars in revenue. The best-selling vehicle in America for over four decades. That's what was riding on getting this right. And we played it safe.

Ford ended up running something forgettable. Something inter-

---

top of the combustion chamber is shaped like half a sphere. Chrysler marketed this so successfully that "It's got a Hemi" became cultural shorthand for power, even though most people had no idea what it meant.

changeable with every other truck ad. It probably tested well in focus groups. It probably met all the brand guidelines. It definitely didn't make anyone feel anything. Moreover, it definitely didn't sell any trucks that wouldn't have sold anyway.

I can't even remember the campaign that ran. Neither can you. That's what four months of approval layers gets you—perfect invisibility.

Most companies think organizational structure is about control— who reports to whom, who approves what, and who has the corner office. But structure is actually about decision-making. Not how many people have to say yes, but how few people need to be in the room.

Amazon doesn't optimize for consensus. They optimize for the smallest number of informed people who can make a decision and move. Two-pizza teams. Single-threaded leaders. Write the press release first, then build backward from what the customer needs.

Apple doesn't have committees reviewing every design choice. They have Jony Ive saying yes or no. One person who understands the Foundation deeply enough to know what fits and what doesn't.

Ford was stuck in the Static State—not just operationally, but mentally. They'd built an approval process that guaranteed safety from bad decisions. But it also guaranteed they'd never make a bold one. They'd confused their Characteristics (careful and methodical) with their Foundation (American ingenuity and toughness).

Structure means clarity: who owns what, who decides what, and who's accountable for what. When everyone needs to approve something, nobody owns it. When nobody owns it, you get four months of meetings and a forgettable truck ad.

Many companies operate like a restaurant where every waiter serves every table. Seems efficient—anyone can help anyone, maximum flexibility. But what actually happens? Orders get lost. Accountability disappears.

The alternative is single-threaded leadership: one person owns one thing completely. Not partially. Not in committee. Completely.

Here's what I mean when I say Foundations should make the decision for you; when your Foundation clearly defines accountability, you don't waste time asking, "How should we structure this?" or "Who needs to be in the meeting?" The Foundation already points to the owner. Strong Foundations don't trap you in process—they eliminate the need for it. They answer, "Who decides?" so your Principles and Characteristics can evolve without committee paralysis.

This sounds simple until you try it. It means that the person has total authority over their domain. They don't need approval. They don't need consensus. They need judgment, which is why hiring for judgment rather than skills becomes critical.

At Amazon, if you own logistics for the Pacific Northwest, you OWN logistics for the Pacific Northwest. Every decision about how packages move in that region goes through you. You don't need to check with headquarters. You don't need committee approval. You make the call; you own the outcome.

That's a terrifying responsibility. It's also the only way to move fast enough to matter.

Most companies can't do this because they don't trust their people to make big decisions. So they create committees, require approvals, and build consensus. Each layer of oversight adds days or weeks. By the time a decision is made, the opportunity has passed.

Amazon's organizational structure goes roughly twelve levels deep— from L1 hourly workers through L12 senior executives. That sounds like the opposite of flat. But there are zero dotted lines. Zero. Every person has one boss. Every decision has one owner. When you're in the room, you can make the final decision. No checking with corporate. No running it up the flagpole. No consensus building.

Most corporate hires start around L4 or L5. Engineers progress from L4 (entry-level) through L6 (senior) and beyond. L8 is Global Director level, running huge global businesses with immense customer and revenue impact. In most Fortune 500 companies, L8 is Chief of Something. Level 9 doesn't exist to make the jump from L8 to L10 (VP) hard. The very top—L11, L12—that's Amazon C-suite territory, rare air.

At every single level, you own your domain completely.

That's the paradox: Amazon has this deep hierarchy but operates as if it is flat because of single-threaded ownership. You can have twelve levels and still move fast if each level has complete authority over their piece.

When I started at Amazon, my boss had nine direct reports. This seemed insane coming from agencies where four to six was standard at a C-level, and two to three at a lower level. Then I understood the genius.

Three direct reports? You can micromanage. Nine direct reports? You can't. You can review every decision, approve every action, and control every output. When you have eight or nine direct reports, you physically can't. You're forced to hire people you trust and let them operate independently.

This is organizational velocity—how fast your flywheel spins.

Think of it this way: if you have three direct reports and you review twenty decisions per day, your maximum organizational velocity is sixty decisions daily. But if you have nine direct reports who each make twenty decisions independently, you've just increased your organizational velocity to 180 decisions daily. Your wheel spins three times faster.

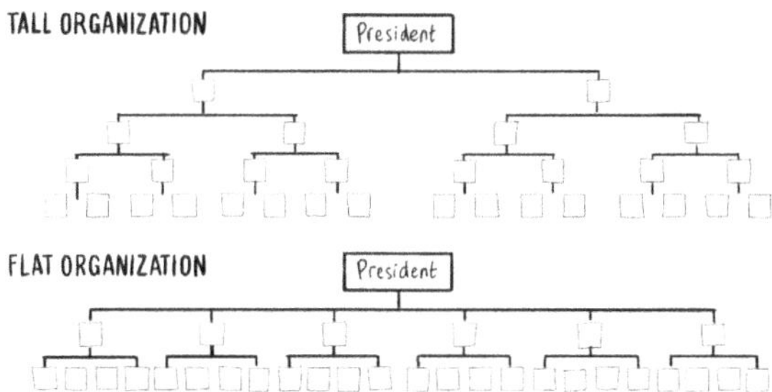

The number of direct reports determines your maximum spin rate. Fewer reports mean more control but slower velocity. More reports mean less control but exponentially faster movement. For organizations that need to explore, experiment, and move at market speed, velocity wins every time.

This only works if you hire people who can actually make decisions. Most people have been trained their entire careers to seek approval, to build consensus, and to minimize risk. Finding people who will take ownership without permission is rare. But it's the only way to build an organization that moves faster than its competition.

Every dotted line on an org chart is a decision that will take three times longer than it should. Dotted lines mean multiple stakeholders. Multiple stakeholders mean alignment meetings. Alignment meetings mean delay.

I watched this destroy a project at WPP, once the world's largest advertising agency holding group and the world's biggest buyer of media. We had a digital transformation initiative with one official owner but dotted lines to finance, IT, HR, and operations. Every decision required a steering committee. Every steering committee required pre-meetings. Every pre-meeting required pre-alignment.

Six months in, we'd had forty-seven meetings and made exactly three decisions. The official owner spent 80% of their time managing stakeholders instead of driving transformation. Eventually, they quit. The project died. The dotted lines remained.

If you want to understand why WPP's stock price collapsed over the past decade—from over $100 per share to under $40—look at how many dotted lines they added to their org charts. Each one slowed their velocity while their digital-native competitors moved at startup speed.

Single-threaded leadership eliminates this. When something goes wrong, you know exactly who to talk to. When something needs to change, one person can make that call.

This is what many companies get wrong: they give people responsibility without authority. You're responsible for growing revenue, but can't set prices. You're responsible for customer satisfaction, but can't change policies. You're responsible for innovation, but can't allocate resources.

This mismatch creates learned helplessness. People stop trying to solve problems because they know they lack the authority to implement solutions. They become professional excuse-makers instead of problem-solvers.

However, there's something worse than giving responsibility without authority: requiring consensus before action.

Everyone having a say is killing innovation, growth, and entire companies.

I don't believe everyone should have a say. Here's why: too many voices water down ideas into consensus mush. When consensus rules, the innovation, direction, strategy, or business becomes flat—vanilla. And vanilla doesn't move the needle.

Think about what happens in a meeting of ten people versus twenty people deciding on a new product direction. With ten people, you might get five distinct viewpoints and one strong direction that emerges. With twenty people, you get twenty opinions, endless debate, and eventually a solution that offends nobody and excites nobody.

The math of consensus is brutal: More inputs = More compromise = Less boldness = Lower impact.

We're not in business to make team members feel good. We're in business to help them grow, to solve customer problems, and to create value. Sometimes that requires making decisions that not everyone agrees with. Sometimes it requires someone to say, "I've heard your input, and here's what we're doing."

The most dangerous trend accelerating this problem? AI.

AI is flattening the world. It's group consensus at its best—and it can kill innovation. When you ask ChatGPT for a strategy, you get the average of everything ever written about that topic. You get conventional wisdom. You get safe. You get what everyone else would also get.

AI is a tool for optimization, not exploration. It's brilliant at finding the center of existing thought. It's terrible at pushing boundaries. If you let AI drive your strategy, you're guaranteeing that you'll be average, because AI is trained on averages.[2]

---

2. This critique applies specifically to generic AI chat interfaces and how most companies currently deploy AI—as a tool for finding consensus and replicating existing patterns. However, companies like Coca-Cola are demonstrating AI's potential when used strategically. Coke's approach combines AI technology with human creativity,

∼

Single-threaded leadership requires absolute alignment between authority and responsibility. If you own something, you must have the authority to change it. All of it. The budget, the team, the strategy, and the execution. Otherwise, you don't actually own it—you're just a care-taker of someone else's decisions.

At Amazon, when you became the single-threaded leader for an initiative, you got a charter that explicitly stated your authority. You could hire and fire. You could change vendors. You could pivot the strategy. You could kill the project if it wasn't working. That's actual ownership.

Most companies can't do this because HR lacks an understanding of the business your team is in. They apply one-size-fits-all policies across completely different contexts. T

However, the person leading breakthrough AI research needs a different hiring authority than the person managing facilities. The team exploring new markets needs different budget flexibility than the team optimizing existing operations.

HR defaults to standardization because it's easier. Equal treatment feels fair. Except it's not fair—it's equally restrictive. It treats A-players and C-players the same. It treats exploratory initiatives and optimization work the same. It treats unique problems with generic solutions.

When I tried to implement wall reviews at WPP—putting our work up every Tuesday and Thursday for open critique—HR pulled me aside after a few months. "You need to slow down," they said. "People aren't comfortable with this level of transparency."

"Don't we want to be good?" I asked.

"But do we need to be?"

That's when I knew something was broken. When HR's job becomes protecting people from excellence instead of enabling it,

---

using it to push creative boundaries rather than settle for the average. The distinction: ChatGPT searching for "what worked before" versus custom AI systems designed to explore "what could work differently." The former guarantees convergence. The latter, when paired with human judgment and clear Foundation, can enable exploration. The risk isn't AI itself—it's using AI to replace thinking instead of augmenting it.

you're no longer in the growth business. You're in the comfort business.

~

PowerPoints are where thinking goes to die. Bullet points let you skip logical connections. Animations distract from weak arguments. Presenting creates performance rather than analysis.

Amazon banned PowerPoints. As I said, every meeting starts with a written narrative—complete thoughts in complete sentences. Six pages, Times New Roman, double-sided, no exceptions. No creativity in format. No hiding behind design. Just thinking made visible.

These documents take weeks, sometimes months to write. That's the point. One person owns it, but they're pulling inputs from everywhere—data teams, finance, engineering, strategy and so on. They're synthesizing conversations, reconciling conflicting viewpoints, and pressure-testing assumptions. You can't fake your way through six pages of prose. You can't hand-wave past the weak parts. You have to think through your entire argument from beginning to end; when finance challenges your numbers, or engineering questions your timeline, you'd better have answers. The document becomes the forcing function for actually understanding what you're proposing.

When everyone reads the same document in silence at the start of a meeting, something remarkable happens. No one's performing. No one's reacting to whoever speaks first. Everyone's processing the same information simultaneously. The discussion then begins from a place of shared understanding.

When thinking is clear, decisions are fast. When everyone understands the logic, implementation is smooth. When assumptions are explicit, problems surface quickly.

The twenty to forty minutes of silent reading that start every Amazon meeting seem inefficient. However, it's actually the most efficient thing you can do. It eliminates the need for pre-reads nobody actually does. It prevents the political theater of presentations. It forces intellectual honesty that PowerPoints actively prevent.

Amazon moves fast by moving slowly where it matters. Those

famous six-page narrative memos? They take weeks, sometimes months to write. They're deep, rigorous documents that force clarity before action. They become the roadmap to work backward from—the Foundation that makes everything else move faster.

The speed doesn't come from skipping thinking. It comes from doing the hard thinking once, getting it right, and then executing without constant renegotiation. The memo process eliminates the endless cycle of meetings to discuss what to discuss, decisions that get revisited, and strategies that shift every quarter because they were never clearly defined in the first place.

Most companies confuse motion with progress. They move fast on everything and slow on nothing. Amazon inverts this: slow on strategy, fast on execution. Rigorous on Foundations, rapid on Characteristics.

Case Study: AWS

Amazon Web Services started as a single-threaded initiative under Andy Jassy. Not a committee. Not a task force. One person with complete authority to build something that didn't exist.

Jassy didn't need to check with retail. He didn't need approval from the board for every decision. He didn't need consensus from other divisions. He had a charter, a budget, and complete authority to execute.

This allowed AWS to operate at startup speed, despite being part of a public company. When customers needed something, Jassy's team built it. When the strategy needed to pivot, they pivoted. When they needed to hire specialized talent, they hired.

The retail side of Amazon thought AWS was a distraction. Many board members questioned why an e-commerce company was building cloud infrastructure. If AWS had been run by committee, if it had required consensus, and if it had dotted lines to every stakeholder, it would have died in meetings.

Instead, single-threaded leadership let AWS grow from an internal tool to a $100 billion business that's worth more than all of Amazon's retail operations combined. One owner. Total authority. No committees.

Watch what happens when companies abandon single-threaded leadership. They create "shared accountability" models where everyone's responsible, so no one's accountable. They establish "tiger teams" with representatives from every department. They form "centers of excellence" that coordinate but don't own.

These structures feel safer. More people have an input. More perspectives are considered. More stakeholders are aligned. But nothing actually happens. Every decision is discussed to death. Every initiative is watered down to consensus. Every bold idea is averaged into adequacy.

I saw this at a CPG company that tried to launch a direct-to-consumer brand. Instead of appointing one owner, they created a "D2C Council" with representatives from sales, marketing, supply chain, finance, IT, and legal. Fifteen people who all had to agree before anything happened.

Eighteen months later, they still hadn't launched. They had beautiful PowerPoints. They had comprehensive project plans. They had stakeholder alignment. What they didn't have was a single person who could say, "We're doing this" and make it happen.

A startup would have launched in six weeks. However, the CPG company needed consensus, and consensus takes time; time, in turn, kills momentum, and dead momentum kills initiatives.

People think flat organizations mean everyone is equal. That's wrong.

They actually require more structure, not less. More discipline, not less. More clarity, not less.

Removing management layers changes how coordination happens. It doesn't eliminate the need. Instead of coordination through hierarchy, you need coordination through systems.

Implementing single-threaded leadership requires three commitments:

First, stop hiring people who need permission. Start hiring people who take ownership. In interviews, ask, "Tell me about a time you made a significant decision without approval." If they can't answer, they're not ready for single-threaded leadership.

Second, you must accept failure in a different way. Real authority creates real mistakes. Some will be expensive. Learn from mistakes quickly. Don't try to prevent them all. A single-threaded leader who fails fast and learns quickly is more valuable than a committee that never fails because it never acts.

Third, you must measure differently. Stop measuring compliance with the process. Start measuring the velocity of decision-making. Stop tracking the number of stakeholders consulted. Start tracking how fast you go from problem to solution. Stop rewarding consensus. Start rewarding conviction.

The world moves fast enough that a startup can beat you to market before your deck is finished. And one bad moment online can undo years of brand building. That's the reality in which we're operating. In a fast-moving world, perfect becomes the enemy of progress.

You can tell your structure actually creates speed when ideas turn into experiments in weeks, decisions happen in one meeting, and people stop asking for permission because they already know what the right thing is.

You know your structure prevents speed when everything requires multiple approvals, meetings are about planning other meetings, people wait for permission rather than forgiveness, and the same discussions happen repeatedly without resolution.

In a flat structure with single-threaded leadership, that F-150 idea would have lived or died in days, not months. One person would have made the call. We would have learned faster, adapted quicker, and moved on to the next idea while our competitors were still in meetings debating whether "mankind" was too gendered.

The F-150 campaign that died in four months of approvals? A startup would have tested it in two weeks, learned it didn't work, and moved on to something better. Or learned it did work and owned the market while Ford was still in committee.

The world moves fast. You either keep up or you fall behind.

The teams that survive aren't chanting "move fast" in all-hands. They've built an environment where slow simply can't happen—because someone owns every decision, and that someone is allowed to make the call without begging three layers of management for permission.

The cost of a wrong decision you can quickly correct is nothing compared to the cost of a slow decision, or worse, no decision at all. Single-threaded leadership isn't just an organizational model. It's a bet that speed and ownership consistently outperform consensus and control.

Strategy and resources mean nothing without execution. Structure creates velocity. And velocity, in a world that moves this fast, is everything.

Speed isn't just about moving fast—it's about having the organizational capability to shift between Explorer and Static States fluidly. Single-threaded leadership isn't just an efficiency play—it's Explorer State infrastructure—because companies stuck in Static State with Static State structures will never escape their own gravity."

15

MAKING THINKING VISIBLE

Brainstorms will fail where wall reviews succeed.

I hate brainstorms. They're probably the biggest waste of time in all of business.

At Amazon, we put five creative teams in a room—ten people total—and gave them the same problem. After forty-five minutes of brainstorming, we had maybe five decent ideas. Most of them safe. All of them obvious.

The loudest person in the room had dominated the conversation. Everyone else had either agreed or stayed quiet. The junior people said nothing. The senior people said everything. We'd spent forty-five minutes performing creativity rather than actually being creative. A week later, we took those same teams and split them into pairs. The same problem, but now with five groups of two people each, working separately. Thirty minutes. Come back with your top ideas.

The difference was profound. Fifty ideas instead of five. Bold concepts instead of safe consensus. Actual solutions instead of theatrical discussion. And all zero groupthink.

In larger brainstorms, the junior designer with the breakthrough idea stays silent because she doesn't want to contradict her boss. The engineer who sees the fatal flaw doesn't speak up because she doesn't want to be negative. The quiet strategist who actually understands the customer never gets a word in because extroverts fill every silence.

We tell ourselves that brainstorms are democratic, and that the best idea wins. That's fantasy. The loudest idea wins. The safest idea wins. The idea that doesn't threaten anyone's ego wins.

This dynamic gets worse with hierarchy. If you're a junior person who's smart but quiet, you're not going to challenge your boss in front of everyone. Your mortgage depends on that job. Your visa might depend on that job. So you nod along while bad ideas get momentum and good ideas evaporate.

I watched this happen constantly in agencies. We'd gather fifteen people in a room, order pizza, put Post-it notes on the walls, and pretend we were innovating. Three hours later, we'd have exactly what the creative director wanted from the beginning, just with everyone else's fingerprints on it so they felt involved.

Pairs change everything. There's nowhere to hide, so both people must contribute. There's no audience to perform for, so you can actually think. There's no hierarchy to navigate, so ideas flow freely.

You can be wrong without being embarrassed. You can build on each other's thinking without competing for airtime. You can go deep on an idea without someone jumping in with their own agenda.

Five pairs working for thirty minutes gives you five times the exploration space of one group. Each pair can pursue different directions without groupthink pulling them back to the middle. Bad ideas die quickly because there's no social pressure to pretend they're good. Good ideas develop because there's time actually to explore them.

More importantly, pairs create intellectual intimacy. When it's just two people, you can admit you don't understand something. You can ask stupid questions. You can think out loud without worrying about looking smart.

When I need to generate ideas, I draw a grid on paper. Two lines horizontal, three lines vertical. Twelve boxes. Each box gets one idea. No explanation, no development, just the core concept.

The constraint is crucial. When you have to fill 12 boxes, you can't fall in love with your first idea. You can't spend twenty minutes perfecting one concept while ignoring eleven others. You must keep moving.

Box one might be obvious. Box two, a slight variation. By box seven, you're getting weird. By box 10, you're in territory you never would have explored if you'd stopped at the first decent idea.

The grid forces breadth before depth. Most business problems are solved in the same way because we delve into the first acceptable solution. We spend weeks developing an idea that should have been abandoned in minutes. The grid won't let you do that. It demands that you explore the entire landscape before settling on a destination.

Boston Consulting Group had already been working on the Axe problem for six months. They'd assembled a team of twelve consultants, including two partners billing at $2,500 per hour. Their final deliverable was a 147-slide PowerPoint that cost Unilever approximately $3.2 million.

Their process was textbook consulting theater. Six weeks of stakeholder interviews, where they asked Unilever executives what they already knew. Four weeks of market analysis, pulling data Unilever already had. Three weeks of competitive benchmarking comparing Axe to Old Spice, Dove Men, and Gillette. Two weeks of consumer segmentation, dividing young men into categories. And finally, three weeks of strategic synthesis arrived at recommendations that surprised no one.

Their conclusion: target urban professional men aged 25-34, position Axe as a premium accessible brand, and focus messaging on confidence through control. They conducted regression analyses that showed a correlation between income and deodorant spending. They had heat maps of purchase behavior. They had a 2x2 matrix plotting brands on axes of functional vs. emotional and mass vs. premium.

Every slide was bulletproof. Every recommendation was defensible. Every decision could be traced to data. It was exactly what you'd expect from paying BCG $3.2 million.

Meanwhile, our Amazon team spent three hours and zero dollars arriving at something completely different.

The contrast in process was stark. While BCG had twelve consultants in conference rooms analyzing spreadsheets, we had five pairs of people with paper and pens. While they spent weeks on stakeholder alignment, we spent thirty minutes in deliberate isolation. While they optimized for consensus and defensibility, we optimized for range and possibility.

Our pairs generated ideas that BCG's process could never produce.

The junior designer and data analyst—the quietest pair who BCG would never have put in a room with Unilever executives—had written something that stopped everyone: stop pretending it's about odor. It's about confidence. Sell the feeling, not the function.

BCG's framework couldn't arrive at this insight because their entire process was built on category conventions. They analyzed what successful deodorant brands did and recommended that Axe do it slightly better. They analyzed purchase data and recommended targeting individuals who were already making purchases. They studied the category and recommended competing within it.

We found something different through forced creative exploration. When you have to fill twelve boxes, you can't just repeat category wisdom. By box seven, you're questioning whether deodorant even needs to be about deodorant. By box twelve, you're in territory that makes people uncomfortable—which is exactly where breakthroughs live.

When we reconvened our pairs, the energy was different from any BCG presentation. We weren't defending recommendations; we were building on possibilities. The subscription idea evolved into a comprehensive direct-to-consumer strategy that would eliminate the need for retail altogether. The confidence positioning became a campaign that admitted what every teenage boy actually thinks: we know why you're buying this, and it's not just about smelling good.

Unilever tested our concepts against BCG's recommendation in matched markets. BCG's premium accessible positioning delivered a 7% lift—exactly what their models predicted. Our confidence subscription concept delivered a 43% lift in trial and three times the retention rate. The campaign that acknowledged insecurity instead of hiding it became Axe's most successful launch in five years.

The difference wasn't due to talent, resources, or even time. BCG had better data, more experience, fancier frameworks, and a hundred times our budget. The difference was in the method. They optimized for the defensible answer. We explored the uncomfortable truth.

Three hours and five pairs of people with paper beat six months and twelve consultants with spreadsheets. Not because we were smarter, but because we had a process that forced exploration beyond the obvious, beyond the safe, beyond what any client would approve without first being made uncomfortable.

Whether it's BCG, McKinsey, KPMG, or any of the other big consulting firms, I do believe that, at their core, firms like Accenture and Deloitte have an incredible amount to offer companies, and they have really steered the ship in many, many ways for many large and small firms over the years. Through AI, I believe they will ultimately render themselves obsolete in the long run, or their business will have to pivot in some way.

They are known for creating extensive, 100-plus-page PowerPoint decks. They're very, very good at prophesying and giving a clear direction on what it should do. Where these larger consulting firms have struggled is in implementation. They pay very well for people who lack extensive experience. Generally speaking (and I know I may receive a lot of criticism for saying this, but it is my opinion), MBAs are taught to think this way, down a particular funnel. They're never taught to think broadly. They're not trained to think what-if questions, and they're generally not taught to do things differently.

This is the problem with most consulting engagements: by the time you see the deck, the thinking is done. They've done the research, formed the conclusions, and built the recommendations. You're reviewing finished thinking, not participating in actual thinking.

That's the model. They go away, analyze, synthesize, polish, and then present. By design, you're brought in at the end. The deck looks impressive. The logic is airtight. The recommendations are clear. But you weren't in the room when they decided which questions mattered. You didn't see what they considered and rejected. You don't know why they went left instead of right at the critical fork. You're being sold a conclusion, not invited into a process.

I'm not saying consulting doesn't have value. Sometimes you need external expertise. Sometimes you need someone who's seen the problem a hundred times before. Sometimes you need the answer, not the process.

However, if you need your team to think differently, to own the solution, and to understand why one direction is better than another, there's a better way.

One of the most powerful mechanisms I've encountered came from watching how Apple and Airbnb operate: wall reviews. Open, regularly scheduled critiques where work literally goes on the wall for everyone to see, discuss, and improve. These are democratic forums where the best idea wins, regardless of who presents it. They replace hidden decks and political maneuvering with open collaboration.

Wall reviews work because they make thinking visible early. When work goes on the wall at 70% done, you're not reviewing execution—you're reviewing direction. You can course-correct before resources are wasted, before egos are invested, and before it's too late to change.

Consulting decks show you finished thinking. Wall reviews show you active thinking. One creates theater. The other creates dialogue. And dialogue is where the actual thinking happens.

They break down silos completely. When ideas are shared openly, people stop protecting turf and start co-creating solutions. Marketing sees what product is building. Product sees what sales is promising. Sales sees what creative is making. Everyone moves in the same direction.

Most leaders say they want great work, but what's their system for getting it? One-on-one reviews behind closed doors? Berating people in groups? Rewarding only the final output when it's too late to improve it? Wall reviews create a system where excellence is inevitable.

After years of testing different approaches, these are my tried and true recommendations for generating breakthrough creative thinking:

Work in pairs, not groups. Two people create intellectual intimacy. Ten people create a performance theater. Split your teams into pairs, give them the same problem, and have them reunite to share their solutions. You'll get five times the ideas in half the time.

Use constraints to force range. The twelve-box grid. Thirty-minute timers. One idea per box, no explanations. Constraints prevent you from falling in love with your first idea. They force you to explore the entire landscape before choosing a destination.

Make thinking visible early and often. Wall reviews. Work is 70% done. Public critique, not private politics. When everyone can see the work, everyone can make it better. When work hides in presentations, it dies in committees.

Leaders speak last. The most senior person should be the last to offer opinions. Feed your team before you feed yourself. Listen before you lead. Let ideas develop before you direct them.

Measure creative velocity, not just output. How many experiments did you run? How many ideas did you kill? How fast did you go from concept to test? You need to have more ideas, faster, with quicker learning cycles.

Wall reviews are the antidote to creative theater. They force real work into real light where real critique can make it better. No hiding behind PowerPoints. No performing confidence. No political maneuvering. Just work on the wall and have an honest conversation about how to improve it.

Just as creative thinking doesn't happen in committees, it doesn't happen in brainstorms. It doesn't happen in PowerPoints. It happens in pairs where there's nowhere to hide. It happens in grids where you're forced past the obvious. And it happens on walls where thinking becomes visible and improvement becomes inevitable.

16

THE VIRTUE OF EMPTY SPACE

How boredom creates breakthrough thinking.

I remember when WiFi first came to planes. Every executive I knew was thrilled—finally, no more lost productivity at 30,000 feet. We could stay connected, keep working, and never miss an email.

Then something interesting happened. One by one, these same executives stopped logging on. Unless there was an actual emergency or maybe a show to finish, they kept their laptops closed. The WiFi was there, but they weren't using it.

Chuck Porter was one of the most vocal about this. Chuck was one of the founders of Crispin Porter + Bogusky—CP+B—along with Sam Crispin and later Alex Bogusky. Under Porter and Bogusky's leadership, CP+B became Adweek's Agency of the Decade for the 2000s, famous for provocative, digital-first creativity and their philosophy of making "advertising that people seek out, not avoid."

Chuck was adamant about staying offline during flights. He'd tell his teams the same thing: "Plane time is the best time to think. You're protected and defended from all incoming messages and people wanting your time. Defend it."

He was right. Four or five hours of enforced disconnection. No emails. No calls. No Slack messages. Just time to process, to connect dots, and to let your mind wander through problems without the pressure of immediate response.

When I fly now, everything I need to read gets printed out before I board. I read with a pen, making notes in margins, still with a red pen like the ones we used at Amazon. By the time I land, I've had the kind of deep thinking that modern business makes nearly impossible.

This is the advantage of boredom—not emptiness, but strategic space for your brain to do what it does best when you stop forcing it to process.

The algorithm has trained us to be afraid of everything. See enough TikToks of shark attacks and you forget that more people die from collapsing sand holes at the beach. The data stream doesn't give you wisdom—it gives you anxiety in real-time. And anxiety is the opposite of the mental state required for breakthrough thinking.

When I'm not flying, after work, before it gets dark, I take the dog out for a walk. No phone. No podcast. No audiobook. Just forty minutes of walking. That's it. And it's actually a really good experience —which shouldn't be remarkable, but somehow it is.

Being comfortable alone—truly alone, not just physically isolated but mentally unplugged—creates the basis for everything else. You can't defend innovation in your organization if you can't defend forty minutes in your own day. The algorithm has made us afraid of being bored. Afraid of being alone. Afraid of forty minutes with nothing to do. That fear kills innovation.

Marcus Raichle at Washington University was studying brain scans when subjects performed specific tasks, but noticed something odd in the control state—when people were supposedly doing "nothing," their brains were highly active in consistent patterns.[1]

---

1. Marcus E. Raichle et al., "The Brain's Default Mode Network," *Annual Review of Neuroscience* 38 (2015)

This network—which Raichle termed the Default Mode Network—was MORE active during rest than during focused tasks. But it doesn't activate during just any rest. Scrolling Twitter isn't rest. Watching a movie isn't rest. Even meditation isn't quite the same thing.

The Default Mode Network activates during unstimulated boredom—when your mind has nothing to process except its own contents. It's the state you reach staring out of a car window at an unchanging landscape. It's what happens in the shower when your hands are busy but your mind is free. It's what happens at 35,000 feet with no WiFi.

I found this same state during endless miles of ultra-marathon training. Twelve hours on a bike. Running through nights. Your body is working, but your mind is completely free.

I remember running the Hood to Coast relay at the peak of my fitness. Normally, a team consists of twelve runners covering 199 miles from Timberline Lodge on Mount Hood in Oregon (where they shot *The Shining*) to Seaside on the Oregon coast. Each runner takes several legs, five to eight miles at a time. It's enormous fun, running through the night, trading off with teammates.

One year, we decided to run it with six runners instead of twelve. Roughly thirty-three miles per person. We skipped the shorter legs and ran doubles—eleven to fourteen miles at a time, three times each. At 2 AM, deep in the Oregon Coast Range, alone on a gravel road with nothing but your footfall for company, your mind does something different.

The solitude and silence create space for thoughts you'd never have at a desk. Problems you've been wrestling with suddenly resolve themselves. Connections appear between ideas that seemed unrelated. The separation from every noise except your own breathing and footsteps—it still makes me smile thinking about it. That's when the magic happens.

Raichle's 2015 review in the Annual Review of Neuroscience showed this network is responsible for connecting disparate pieces of information into new patterns, processing and consolidating experiences into learning, generating what we experience as creativity and insight, and maintaining our sense of self and continuity over time.

Without boredom, this network never fully activates. Without activation, innovation dies.

Arthur C. Brooks, a Harvard professor studying happiness and meaning, puts it more bluntly: "You need to be bored. You will have less meaning and you will be more depressed if you never are bored."[2] His colleague Dan Gilbert ran experiments where people had to sit in a room for fifteen minutes with nothing to do except push a button that gave them a painful electric shock. Most participants shocked themselves rather than sit with boredom.[3]

We've eliminated boredom from modern life. The phone in your pocket has shut off your Default Mode Network almost completely. Every fifteen-second wait at a traffic light becomes an opportunity to scroll, to check, and to fill the space with anything except your own thoughts.

Brooks calls it "a doom loop of meaning." If every time you're slightly bored you pull out your phone, it gets harder and harder to find meaning. That's the recipe for the explosion of depression and anxiety we're seeing everywhere.

My training stopped at Amazon. Completely. The cycling ended. The running disappeared. The gym sessions that had kept me centered —gone. That should have told me everything. Because when the training stops, the boredom stops. And when the boredom stops, you lose access to the part of your brain that tells you who you are and what matters.

Companies do the same thing. They eliminate boredom from their culture. Every meeting is packed with content. Every moment is scheduled. Every silence is filled with another presentation, another update, or another initiative. The Default Mode Network doesn't just exist in individuals—it exists in organizations.

The best ideas don't come from brainstorming sessions. They come from the shower. From the long run. From staring out the window on a cross-country flight with no WiFi. They come from the spaces between

---

2. Arthur C. Brooks, "You Need to Be Bored. Here's Why," *Harvard Business Review*, August 28, 2025

3. Timothy D. Wilson et al., "Just Think: The Challenges of the Disengaged Mind," *Science* 345, no. 6192 (2014)

the scheduled work, when your mind is free to make connections it would never make under pressure.

When you eliminate boredom from your company culture, you eliminate the cognitive space where innovation actually happens. You get efficiency. You get execution. You get people who are very good at doing what they already know how to do.

What you don't get is the breakthrough insight that changes everything.

Warren Buffett's calendar would shock most executives. While CEOs pack their schedules with back-to-back meetings, Buffett often has just one or two appointments per week. The rest? Reading. Thinking. Sitting in his office in Omaha, doing what looks like nothing.

Bill Gates once compared calendars with Buffett and was stunned. Gates' was packed with five-minute increments. Buffett had entire blank weeks. "You've got to keep control of your time," Buffett told him, "and you can't unless you say no. You can't let people set your agenda in life."

This isn't laziness—it's strategy. Buffett reads 500 pages a day. Not skimming. Not scanning headlines. Deep reading that requires sustained boredom tolerance. "That's how knowledge works," he says. "It builds up, like compound interest."

When Todd Combs was hired to potentially succeed Buffett, Buffett gave him one piece of advice: "Read 500 pages like this every day," pointing to a stack of reports. "All of you can do it, but I guarantee not many of you will do it."

Why won't they? Because five minutes into reading an annual report, their brain screams for stimulation. Their phone buzzes. Their email dings. The boredom feels unbearable, so they choose the dopamine hit of responding to something—anything—rather than sitting with the discomfort of deep focus.

Sandi Mann and Rebekah Cadman at the University of Central Lancashire ran an experiment in 2014 that should be mandatory reading for every innovation team.

They took two groups and gave them a creative challenge: come up with as many uses as possible for two polystyrene cups. But first, one group had to do the most boring task imaginable—copy numbers from a phone book for 15 minutes.

The bored group didn't just outperform the other—they generated solutions the control group never even considered. While the control group suggested obvious uses (pen holder, plant pot), the bored group invented elaborate solutions (earrings, telephones, and Madonna-style bras).

Mann ran variations. Some groups read the phone book instead of copying it—even more boring, even better results. The peak came when subjects had to read the phone book backwards. Maximum boredom produced maximum creativity.

The mechanism is simple: boredom creates a state of profound understimulation. Your brain, desperate for engagement, starts making connections it would never make when occupied. It reaches into distant memories, combines unrelated concepts, and generates novel solutions.

Much of modern work has eliminated every pocket of boredom. We've optimized away the very state that produces breakthrough thinking.

3M's "15% time" policy[4] didn't start as an innovation strategy. It started because managers noticed something odd: their best inventors kept getting caught working on unauthorized projects. Rather than punish them, 3M made it a policy.

However, the 15% time wasn't structured innovation time. It was boredom time. Engineers would sit at their desks, supposedly "thinking about" problems, often appearing to do nothing at all.

Art Fry, inventor of the Post-it Note, spent most of his 15% time in

---

4. Introduced around 1948, the policy, often referred to as "bootlegging" allows employees to spend 15% of their working hours on personal, innovative projects outside their normal assignments.

what he called "daydreaming mode." He'd been in the church choir, getting annoyed that his bookmarks kept falling out of his hymnal. The solution didn't come during focused problem-solving. It came during one of his boredom sessions when his mind connected the bookmark problem with Spencer Silver's "failed" adhesive from years earlier.

The Post-it Note generated over $1 billion in revenue. It came from boredom.

Jeff Bezos doesn't set an alarm. He reads the newspaper in a leisurely manner. He has breakfast with his family. When he was still CEO, his first meeting was never before 10 AM.

"I like to putter in the morning," he told the Economic Club of Washington. "I like to read the newspaper. I like to have coffee. I like to have breakfast with my kids before they go to school."

This is someone who understands that high-quality decisions require a specific mental state. "I do my high-IQ meetings before lunch," Bezos explained. "Like anything that's going to be really mentally challenging, that's a 10 o'clock meeting. And by 5 PM, I'm like, 'I can't think about this today. Let's try this again tomorrow at 10 AM'."

The puttering isn't wasted time—it's preparation. His brain is processing overnight thoughts, making subconscious connections, and preparing for the cognitive load ahead. By the time his first meeting starts, he's had hours of unstimulated thinking.

Compare this to the typical executive who checks email before getting out of bed, rushes through breakfast while scanning news, and arrives at the office already mentally depleted. They've had zero boredom and zero processing time, thus zero space for their Default Mode Network to activate.

Growing up in that Land Rover, driving through the Australian Outback at fifteen miles per hour, I had nothing but boredom. Hours and hours and hours of red dirt, spinifex grass, and the unchanging horizon. No iPad. No iPhone. No screens of any kind. Just the back of my parents' heads and the endless, merciless sameness of the desert.

So my mind wandered. Not occasionally—constantly. I invented elaborate games. I imagined I was skiing behind the car, weaving between obstacles only I could see. I created entire civilizations in the dust patterns on the window. I had conversations with myself, playing multiple characters. I solved problems that didn't exist. I asked questions that had no answers.

That mental wandering wasn't empty time—it was training. My brain was learning to entertain itself, to make connections between unrelated things, and to find patterns in chaos. The boredom wasn't just building creativity; it was building the capacity for sustained thought.

This early training in boredom tolerance shaped everything that came after. The ability to sit through brutal Amazon meetings where nothing seemed to happen for hours. The patience to work on campaigns for months before seeing results. The mental stamina to push through the twentieth iteration when everyone else wanted to quit at the tenth.

How to strategically deploy boredom:

No-Meeting Mornings: Block the first two hours of every day. No meetings, no calls, and no Slack. This isn't focus time—it's processing time.

Walking Meetings Without Agendas: Steve Jobs did this. He just walked, and problems got discussed without the pressure to solve them.

Mandatory Disconnection: Microsoft Japan experimented with a four-day workweek. Productivity jumped 40%. It was not because people worked harder in four days—it was because the three-day weekend gave their brains time to process and reset.

The Phone Book Exercise: Before major creative sessions, give teams genuinely boring tasks for 15 minutes. Not fake boring like organizing files. Truly boring like reading terms and conditions or copying random numbers.

The human brain evolved over millions of years with abundant boredom. Hours watching horizons, tending fires, and walking between destinations. This boredom wasn't a bug—it was a feature. It's when our brains consolidate learning, generate insights, and prepare for challenges.

We've spent twenty years eliminating every moment of boredom. However, boredom is like sleep—you can skip it for a while, but eventually the debt comes due. Declining innovation. Employee burnout. The gradual loss of deep thinking capability.

The solution isn't abandoning technology or returning to the Outback. It's strategically reintroducing boredom into your systems. Protecting empty space as fiercely as you protect productive time. Understanding that doing nothing is sometimes the most important thing you can do.

I protect my thinking time religiously. Not because I am avoiding work—because that empty space is where the work actually happens. The Default Mode Network is being activated. The brain is doing what it evolved to do.

Next time you feel bored, resist the urge to reach for your phone. Sit with it. Let your mind wander. Let the discomfort happen. Given my background, I can turn boredom on easily. But anyone can find it if they try.

That discomfort you feel? That's your brain preparing to do something brilliant.

You just have to give it the space.

17

WHEN HR BECOMES THE ENGINE

Transforming HR from Enemy to Engine.

In most companies, Human Resources has become the chief architect of the Static State. It is the department that says no, the champion of standardization, and the defender of comfortable mediocrity. It will sacrifice millions in value to enforce a policy from a spreadsheet. I'm going to show you why this obsession with compliance is killing your growth, and how the best companies—like Amazon with its Bar Raisers—treat HR not as a policy enforcement unit, but as the fiercely protective engine that embeds the Core Foundation into every person and decision.

Recently, at a major advertising agency holding company, one of its top executives relocated from Seattle to Milwaukee. This was a behind-the-scenes operator who maintained tight relationships and kept global projects moving forward. They had been keeping multiple eight-figure accounts happy—the kind of accounts that keep agencies alive with a steady tick of revenue. The client covered 100% of their salary, 100% of the travel, so the agency wasn't even paying for them.

However, the agency's HR team wanted to reduce their pay by 24% due to the relocation.

Their logic? Wisconsin salaries should be lower than those in Washington. They had spreadsheets. They had cost-of-living calculations. They had market data. What they didn't have was any understanding of how business actually works.

HR had pushed aside all the effort, all the commitment, and all the value—and stripped it to an Excel spreadsheet.

The employee went straight to the C-suite at one of the client's companies. The executives couldn't understand what the problem was; they were furious. Why would you punish someone who's delivering exactly what you need? However, the agency's HR had already spent weeks building their case. They had their frameworks. They had their policies. They were going to die on this hill. They were dying because of a policy. A policy, not a person.

HR sees people as policies to enforce.

This is the Static State in perfect miniature: an organization so obsessed with internal fairness that it will actively destroy value in the name of process, where spreadsheets matter more than relationships, where policy trumps performance. And where being "right," according to the handbook, means losing millions in revenue.

This same blindness shows up in how companies hire senior executives. One of the biggest problems I've consistently seen is organizations bringing in senior leaders without any clear charter for what they're supposed to do.

There's a job description—sure. Some bullet points about responsibilities, required experience, and reporting structure. But a charter is clarity about what you're actually being hired to achieve. Are you here to explore new territory? Or to consolidate what exists? To blow things up and rebuild? Or to steady the ship through rough waters?

Without that clarity, talented leaders flounder. They come in with energy and ideas, but no one's told them whether they're supposed to be an Explorer or a Static State operator. Should they be taking risks or reducing them? Building new capabilities or optimizing current ones? Changing everything or changing nothing?

I've watched brilliant executives fail, not because they lacked capability, but because they were never told what game they were playing. The board wanted transformation but hired someone to maintain. The CEO wanted maintenance but hired someone to transform. Six months in, everyone's frustrated. The executive feels constrained. Leadership feels disappointed. And the executive leaves for "a better opportunity" —which usually just means a place with a clearer charter.

The companies that get this right are explicit from day one. When Amazon hires a senior leader, they know whether they're hiring an Explorer or an operator. When they brought in executives to build AWS, the charter was clear: create an entirely new business. When they hire for retail operations, the charter is different: make the best system better.

A scope can be rebuilt, redesigned, or kept at the status quo. But if you're not clear which one you want, your best leaders will leave. They won't leave because they failed, but because you never told them what success looked like.

Based on the Under Armour example earlier in the book, Kevin Plank should have empowered or hired an operational leader to "protect the house" while he continued to explore. Being super clear why you're hiring someone, what they need to do, and what they need to achieve—before you hire—is imperative.

Before we solve the HR problem, you need to understand what you're actually managing.

Every year, companies send out employee satisfaction surveys. And every year, HR treats the results like they're measuring one number across the entire organization. Everyone gets lumped together. Everyone gets averaged out. The whole company gets a 6.7 out of 10, and HR builds programs to move that to a 7.2.

If you want growth, you can't do that.

One in three employees doesn't trust their direct leader. That's the average. But the range is broad, depending on what work they do.

In retail and hospitality? One in two people distrusts their boss. The stress, the customer-facing chaos, the low autonomy—it creates friction with leadership that's almost structural.

In finance and professional services? One in five. They might not love you, but they respect competence. They're there for the work, not the emotional connection.

Creative and marketing teams fall somewhere in between—about 35-40% distrust. Those who rely more on EQ are more sensitive to recognition, to leadership style, and to whether you actually understand what we do. Emotional connection matters more than hierarchy for this group.

Engagement tells an even worse story. Only about 30% of employees are actually engaged—involved, enthusiastic, and giving a damn. Another 60% are just showing up. Not energized, not excited, just...there. And about 15% are actively disengaged—the ones who undermine others, erode morale, and poison the culture.

Half your team is open to leaving for another job. Right now. Not because they hate you—just because they're keeping their options open.

From my experience, the people who complain the most—who complete negative satisfaction surveys and grumble about the culture —are usually the B and C performers. They always stay because it's easy and they want comfort. They're okay complaining, because that's what keeps them there. They get little attention because, frankly, they're not worth it.

Meanwhile, your A players either thrive in the culture or leave quickly if it doesn't fit – worse, they are often tired of the lower performers consistently underperforming, and that's why they leave. The complainers? They're the barnacles on your ship, creating drag and never contributing to forward motion.

Here's the simplified version—call it The 30-60-50 Rule:

For every 10 people on your team, three resist your style, three coast in the middle, and three are eyeing the door.

Traditional HR tries to make all 10 equally satisfied. They treat everyone like one number. They create policies that optimize for the average. In doing so, they lose the best people while protecting the worst.

A good HR team does something different. They focus on moving one or two people at a time toward trust and clarity. They recognize that a retail manager and a software engineer experience leadership completely differently. A creative and a finance analyst need different things from their boss.

When you treat people like a number, they become a number.

During my Amazon interview process, the interviewer asked me to stand up, walk to the whiteboard, and diagram how I'd solve a specific customer problem. Not present a solution I'd prepared. Not talk through my thinking. Actually draw it out, live, while explaining my reasoning.

I fumbled. I drew boxes and arrows that made no sense. I erased and started over twice. It was uncomfortable and messy and nothing like the polished presentations I was used to giving.

That was precisely the point.

Amazon wasn't testing my ability to present. They were testing my ability to think. To work through ambiguity in real-time. To be vulnerable and transparent when I didn't have all the answers. Because that's what the actual job required every single day.

One question from that interview was: "Tell me about a time you had the data to prove you were right, but you chose to be wrong."

I didn't understand the question. How could you choose to be wrong if the data proved you were right?

The interviewer clarified: "Sometimes being right destroys trust. Sometimes being right breaks relationships you need for long-term success. Sometimes being right means missing the bigger picture. Tell me about a time you understood this."

That question revealed Amazon's true priorities. They weren't hiring people who could win arguments. They were hiring people who could build systems.

My friend Tom, who told me the coffee table book story we covered in Moments that Matter, explained it to me later: "Jeff never hired for skills. He hired for judgment. You can teach someone to code, write, or analyze. You can't teach them when to ignore the data and trust their gut. You can't teach them when being technically correct is actually being fundamentally wrong."

Most companies hire for what people have done. Amazon hired for how people think. Most companies want proof of past success. Amazon wanted evidence of future judgment.

Amazon's Bar Raiser program is the most sophisticated hiring mechanism I've encountered. Every significant hire requires a Bar Raiser—someone from a completely different part of the organization who has no stake in filling the position quickly.

The Bar Raiser has one job: protecting Amazon's culture. They can veto any hire. Period.

It doesn't matter if the hiring manager is desperate. It doesn't matter if the candidate is brilliant. If the Bar Raiser says no, the answer is no. Their only question: will this person raise the bar or lower it?

This seems crazy. Jobs stay empty. Managers get frustrated. But it prevents death by a thousand compromises.

You hire one person who's "good enough." Now they have become the new standard. The next hire only has to be as good as them. Then the next. Then the next. After a hundred hires, your company is entirely different—weaker, slower, and more average.

But Amazon went further. They made their Principles real by building them into everything.

It's a specific question in every interview: "Tell me about a time you went against what was best for your team because it was best for the customer." You can't fake it. You need real examples with real outcomes.

Ownership is measured: "When have you taken responsibility for something that wasn't your job?" No example, no hire. No exceptions.

These are requirements. You cannot be hired, promoted, or

rewarded at Amazon without demonstrating that you live by these Principles.

That's the difference between Principles and decoration. Principles have teeth. They bite. They cost you good candidates who don't fit. They slow down hiring. They make things harder.

However, they also ensure that ten years later, you're still the same company—just bigger, not different.

Moreover, here's something I learned later: the best HR business partners I've had—the ones who actually understood this—had all worked in the industry before becoming talent leaders. They understood the actual work, not just the policies surrounding it. They knew what good looked like because they'd done it themselves.

Modern HR thinks its job is to minimize risk, standardize compensation, and ensure compliance. They've become the department that says no. No to exceptional compensation for exceptional performance. No to different treatment for different value creation. No to anything that might create inequality, even when that inequality reflects reality.

They should be asking: how do we get talented people to do the best work of their lives? How do we remove friction from high performers? How do we make this the place where ambitious people come to build things?

Instead, they're asking: how do we ensure pay equity across regions? How do we standardize performance reviews? How do we make everything perfectly defensible in case we get sued?

That obsession with defensibility is killing companies. Business isn't fair. The person who brings in $50 million in revenue shouldn't be paid the same as someone who brings in $5 million just because they have the same title. But HR can't handle that. They need their frameworks, their bands, and their matrices.

HR's actual job—the job they should be doing—is setting resources free to help brands grow.

If companies grow when people grow, then HR should measure

inputs that help people grow. Amazon gets this. They obsess over inputs, not outputs. How many sales calls did you make? How many customers did you help? How many new capabilities did your team build? Those inputs drive the outputs you want.

However, most companies flip it. They measure revenue and wonder why it's not growing. They measure employee satisfaction and wonder why engagement is dropping. They're watching the scoreboard instead of running the plays.

If HR puts people in a box, people will be in boxes, and so will the thinking. But when HR's role is to unlock capability, to remove obstacles, and to make excellence possible—that's when companies transform.

HR should be the steward of your Foundation—those unchanging values that define why you exist. At Delta, Ed Bastian doesn't just talk about service culture—HR ensures it scales across 90,000 employees. When your Foundation lives only in the CEO's head or the marketing deck, it's vulnerable. One leadership change, one bad quarter, or one activist investor, and it evaporates. But when HR embeds the Foundation into every people process, it becomes institutional, generational, and permanent.

At Delta, Ed Bastian doesn't just talk about service culture—HR ensures it scales across 90,000 employees. They don't process new hires; they indoctrinate them into a belief system where every interaction matters.

At Airbnb, HR doesn't manage talent; they cultivate the sense of belonging that defines the entire brand. Brian Chesky runs weekly design reviews, not because he's a micromanager, but because he's embedding "belonging" into how they hire, how they build, and how they show up. As we saw, when COVID made their business collapse, they didn't panic and hire consultants. They doubled down on their Foundation—near-not-far travel, extended stays, and private homes. HR helped them pivot without losing themselves.

At Apple, you don't get hired unless you demonstrate a genuine obsession with the intersection of technology and liberal arts. Not just interest. Obsession. HR screens for this ruthlessly. They'd rather leave a position open for months than hire someone brilliant who doesn't share a belief in the Foundation.

This seems inefficient until you realize what it prevents: the slow dilution that kills companies from within. Every hire who doesn't share your Foundation weakens it. Compound that over hundreds of hires, and suddenly you're a different company entirely.

Explorer organizations understand that talent is not a resource to be managed but a capability to be unleashed. They don't hire people to fill roles. They hire people to solve problems that haven't been defined yet.

This requires a shift in how we think about talent:

Stop hiring for cultural fit. Start hiring for cultural contribution. You don't need more people who think like you. You need people who think differently but share your values. There's a massive difference between alignment on beliefs and conformity in thinking.

Stop managing performance. Start removing obstacles to performance. Instead of asking, "How do we get more out of people?" Ask, "What's preventing people from doing their best work, and how do we eliminate it?"

Stop standardizing compensation. Start recognizing that different people create vastly different value, and that's okay. The unfairness isn't in paying people differently. The unfairness is in paying them the same when their contributions are vastly different.

Stop protecting people from failure. Start protecting their ability to learn from failure. The goal isn't to prevent mistakes but to ensure mistakes become education rather than career death sentences.

The HR teams that drive growth rather than prevent it understand that Principles without mechanisms are just philosophy. Traditional HR measures time to fill positions, cost per hire, and turnover rates.

The transformation from HR as enemy to HR as engine requires specific mechanisms:

Create Bar Raisers for your Core. Identify people who deeply embody your values—not necessarily your most senior people, but your most culturally aligned. Give them veto power over hires. Yes, this will slow hiring. That's the point. Better to have an empty seat than the wrong person.

Replace competency models with judgment indicators. Stop asking, "Can they do the job?" Start asking, "Can they make good decisions when there's no playbook?" Design interview questions that reveal the thinking process, not just experience.

Replace performance reviews with Impact Reviews. Most performance reviews ask, "How did you perform?" That's backward-looking and subjective. Impact Reviews ask different questions:

What impact did you create for customers? For the team? For the business?

What obstacles did you remove that made others more effective?

What did you build that will outlast your tenure here?

The shift is subtle but profound. Performance measures you. Impact measures what you made possible for others. Performance can be faked with busy work.

Build mechanisms, not policies. A policy says, "treat people fairly." A mechanism makes unfairness structurally impossible. Amazon's Leadership Principles aren't policies—they're mechanisms embedded in every decision. Their PRFAQ documents aren't bureaucracy—they're mechanisms that force customer-centric thinking. These mechanisms protect everybody because there's a customer at the center.

Measure cultural strength, not just performance. Track whether your Foundation is strengthening or diluting. Are new hires raising or lowering the bar? Are decisions reflecting your Principles or contradicting them?

Accept productive inequality. Some people create ten times more value than others. Pay them accordingly. Promote them faster. Give them more resources. The alternative isn't fairness—it's watching your best people leave for companies that recognize their value.

❧

When HR becomes the steward of the Foundation, when they see their role as protecting and strengthening what makes the company special rather than making everything equal, the entire organization will be transformed. Decisions will be made faster because everyone understands the Principles. Talent will be unleashed when obstacles are removed. Culture will be strengthened because every hire reinforces rather than dilutes what you believe.

HR departments that enforce compliance die slowly. HR teams that enable exploration build the future. One creates friction. The other creates fuel. One manages decline. The other drives growth.

Your HR team is either your biggest obstacle or your greatest accelerator. There's no middle ground. They're either protecting what makes you special or slowly destroying it through standardization. They're either the steward of your Foundation or the architect of your convergence toward average.

Instead of asking candidates, "What salary are you looking for?"—which curtails the possibility from the first conversation—they should ask, "What value will you bring to help our customers grow?" Don't use HR as a limiter. Use it as an accelerator.

The shift starts with this recognition: HR is there to protect the company. HR has the company's interests at heart. But that limits people's growth. Surely, when people grow, so does the company. That's the Inputs versus Outputs of Amazon.

Any inputs to help a company grow should be measured. In HR, they handle most companies' most valuable resource—people. But they treat that resource like two-year-olds instead of what they actually are: the engine of everything you're trying to build.

Here's how to actually do it:

1. Name the discomfort. Transparency builds trust faster than pretending everything is fine. When you're implementing change, when you're raising standards, and when you're making work visible—say it out loud. "This is going to be uncomfortable. We're doing it anyway because comfortable companies die slowly."

2. Clarify the next action. Simplicity reduces fear and disengagement. People can handle hard if they know what to do next. They can't handle ambiguity that feels like chaos.

3. Practice micro-truths. Five-minute weekly check-ins: what's working, what's wobbling. Not performance reviews. Not status updates. Actual conversations about actual work.

4. Make discomfort shared. Show that growth is a team muscle, not individual punishment. When everyone's uncomfortable together, it's called progress. When one person is uncomfortable alone, it's called targeted harassment. The difference matters.

5. Reward stretch, not perfection. Celebrate those who lean in and learn, not just those who succeed. The person who tried something bold and failed is more valuable than the person who played it safe and succeeded—because they're building capability for the future.

HR's job isn't to manage people—it's to unleash them.

When HR becomes the engine instead of the brake, everything changes. Hiring becomes about raising the bar, not filling seats. Compensation becomes about recognizing value, not standardizing mediocrity. Culture becomes something you protect fiercely, not something that is diluted with every compromise.

This transformation requires leadership conviction that borders on irrationality. You have to believe that Principles matter more than policies. That judgment matters more than experience. The right person who thinks differently is worth ten people who think the same.

You have to be willing to leave positions empty. To pay people unequally. And to make some people uncomfortable in the service of making everyone better.

That's HR as it should be: the engine that drives everything else.

At the end of the day, your people are either your greatest asset or your biggest liability. There's no middle ground. And the department responsible for those people—HR—determines which one they become.

18

PROTECTED INNOVATION

Creating sanctuaries where breakthrough thinking can survive.

Your organization has an immune system that is programmed to attack and destroy any foreign body. Innovation is a foreign body. This is not a metaphor—it's the reason why every new idea is met with the same antibodies: "What's the ROI? Let's form a committee." I'm going to show you the fatal progression from measurement to death, and how the only way to generate a future is to build protected sanctuaries—bomb shelters for your best ideas—and why this looks like waste, inefficiency, and general craziness to everyone outside the perimeter.

I once worked with a creative agency that wondered why they'd stopped having breakthrough ideas. The answer was hiding in plain sight: timesheets.

Every ten minutes had to be accounted for. Every hour needed a client code. The informal conversations that used to spark genius? Gone. The random explorations that led to unexpected solutions? You can't bill those. The Friday afternoon mess-around sessions where the magic happened? "We need to maximize utilization."

They optimized their creativity to death—measured it until it stopped breathing.

This is usually how it goes. First, someone suggests tracking time "just to understand where it goes." Seems reasonable. Then they want codes for different activities. Still harmless. Then utilization targets appear—80%, then 85%, then 90%. The unallocated time shrinks. The breathing room disappears. Boredom disappears.

Next come the dashboards. Red numbers for underutilization. Weekly reviews of who's below target. Public scoreboards. Suddenly, everyone's at 95% utilization, and nobody can remember the last breakthrough idea.

The agency I worked with had gone from producing culture-changing campaigns to competing on efficiency. They'd become a factory that happened to make ads. Their clients noticed—billings dropped, talent fled, and they couldn't figure out why their "improved processes" had destroyed their product.

This is happening everywhere. Quarterly earnings calls strangle five-year thinking. ROI calculations abort moonshots on the launch pad. Performance reviews punish anyone who fails productively. We've created organizations that demand innovation while systematically destroying the conditions that create it.

The progression is always the same. Measurement leads to optimization. Optimization leads to efficiency. Efficiency leads to death. Not dramatic death—boring death. The kind where you slowly become irrelevant while your dashboards glow green.

Most companies don't protect innovation. They perform it.

They build innovation labs with exposed brick and neon signs. They run hackathons that generate ideas nobody implements. They appoint Chief Innovation Officers who report to the CFO. They create innovation metrics that measure everything except innovation.

I consulted for a Fortune 500 company that spent $20 million on an innovation center. Gorgeous space. Whiteboards everywhere. Meditation rooms. A slide between floors. Know what they didn't have?

Permission to fail. Every project needed a business case. Every experiment needed a projected ROI. Every team needed to justify their existence quarterly.

The space looked like innovation. It had all the props. But when an antibody wearing a suit asked, "What's the return on this?" nobody had protection. The innovation center became the world's most expensive conference room.

This is innovation theater. It makes executives feel progressive without requiring actual change. It lets organizations say, "we innovate" while maintaining the exact structures that prevent innovation.

Real protection doesn't look innovative. It looks like waste. It looks like inefficiency. It looks like people doing nothing productive. That's why it works—the antibodies don't recognize it as a threat until it's too late.

Some organizations have figured out how to build bomb shelters for innovation.

Spotify structures itself into autonomous squads that can ship without permission. They don't submit for approval or align with stakeholders. They ship. Deploy. Learn. No antibodies can form because there's no trigger mechanism to activate them.

Each squad owns their metrics, their decisions, and their failures. The larger organization can't reject what it doesn't control. Protection through autonomy, not through process. But if a squad's mission becomes irrelevant, it disbands. No reassignment to maintain headcount. No pivot to justify existence. Death. This threat of mortality keeps the squads in Explorer State—they can't settle into comfortable inefficiency because comfortable inefficiency is fatal.

Amazon does something different. They protect innovation through writing. No PowerPoints. No pitch decks. Every idea starts as a six-page narrative. A complete thought, fully formed, that has to stand on its own logic.

Written narratives protect ideas from drive-by criticism, from political theater, and from the kind of half-attention that kills innovation in most companies. You can't skim a six-pager. You can't multitask through it. You have to engage or get out.

However the real protection comes from the PRFAQ format—writing the press release first. Before any building, before any investment, teams write the customer announcement. This reverses the antibody response. Instead of defending what you want to build, you're defending what customers will experience. The immune system has a harder time attacking customer value than internal projects.

Each approach is different, but the pattern is clear: Protection isn't a policy. It's architecture. You design innovation into the structure itself, or the antibodies win.

Case Study: The Beatles

The Beatles didn't schedule "Revolution 9" into their calendar. They were messing around with tape loops, and George Martin protected the mess.

That's the part everyone misses. Martin wasn't just their producer. He was their defender. When the studio accountants questioned why the world's biggest band was "wasting" expensive studio time making weird noises, Martin kept them out. When EMI executives wanted more "She Loves You," Martin bought space for experimentation.

Four musicians cutting up physical tape, running it backward, speeding it up, and slowing it down. Hours of "nothing." Days of "waste." Expensive studio time spent making sounds that might never become songs. Martin was standing at the door, telling the label, "They're working."

The mess created *Sergeant Pepper*. The waste produced *The White Album*. The inefficiency revolutionized popular music.

Imagine if EMI had installed productivity metrics. Track songs per studio hour. Measure commercial potential. Optimize hit production. Dashboard everything. The Beatles would have efficiently produced variations on "She Loves You" until they became an oldies act.

Your company isn't a band making experimental music. But that's exactly why you need to study them. The business you're in will only teach you what you already know. Look elsewhere for learning that actually transforms.

Innovation doesn't need managers. It needs defenders.

The defender's job isn't to direct or optimize or measure. It's to maintain the perimeter. To fight off the antibodies. To protect the productive discomfort long enough for something unprecedented to emerge.

Most organizations promote managers and wonder why innovation dies. They put efficiency experts in charge of exploration. They ask the immune system to nurture the very thing it's designed to destroy.

Remember the Convergence Cascade from earlier—how small pressures compound into complete conformity? Protected innovation is the opposite: small freedoms that compound into a breakthrough.

It starts with one protected hour. Nobody can schedule over it. No meetings, no calls, no "quick questions." Just one hour of organizational silence. In that hour, someone has an idea they wouldn't have had in a meeting.

That idea needs a conversation, but not a meeting. So you protect informal collisions—cafeterias that encourage lingering, walking paths that promote discussion, and coffee bars that create congregation. The idea finds a collaborator.

Now two people need space to experiment. Not a lab, just permission to try something without a business case. They build something rough, something embarrassing, something that barely works. But it works.

The prototype needs resources—not approval, resources. The difference is critical. Approval activates antibodies. Resources enable exploration. So you protect a budget that doesn't require justification, time that doesn't demand ROI, and equipment that isn't optimized for utilization.

Each protection layers onto the last. The hour becomes a day. The day becomes a project. The project becomes a product. The product becomes the future.

But remove any layer of protection, and the cascade reverses. The antibodies find a foothold. The innovation dies, and nobody can pinpoint exactly when it happened. All companies need phases in Explorer State. But even companies in Static State need to allow space for Explorer State, because that is where the innovation happens. The danger is when Static State becomes the enemy of Explorer State

Three things kill protected innovation, usually in this order:

New Leadership. The executive who understood why that team needed space leaves. The replacement walks in: "Why are these people just sitting around thinking? What's their output? What's their utilization?" The sanctuary becomes a target.

The new leader isn't evil. They're doing what got them promoted: improving efficiency, maximizing resources, and driving results. They see waste and want to fix it. They see inefficiency and want to optimize it. They're good executives doing their jobs, which is exactly why they're so dangerous.

Success. This is the cruelest killer. The protected innovation actually works. It grows. It needs resources, structure, and process. The thing that needed protection from the organization becomes part of the organization. The Explorer State calcifies into Static State, and nobody notices until it's too late.

I once watched this happen at a tech company. Their skunkworks[1] team created a breakthrough product. Success. Growth. Suddenly, they needed HR policies, budget approvals, and quarterly reviews. The same team that revolutionized an industry couldn't innovate their way out of their own success. Five years later, they were disrupted by a startup doing exactly what they used to do.

Efficiency Creep. It starts innocently. "Just this quarter, we need all hands on deck." Then: "Can we borrow a few people from the innovation lab?" Then: "Times are tight, we need to maximize resources."

---

1. Skunkworks meaning a a small, loosely structured, often secretive group within an organization that is tasked with developing innovative or experimental projects.

Watch what happens to headcount. The creative groups get trimmed. The innovation teams get "right-sized." People get pulled from the groups that protect the company's future and reassigned to optimize the present.

When you move headcount out of innovation, you're saying: "I don't care about the future."

The protected space gets colonized six minutes at a time. One meeting here. One fire drill there. One "quick project" that turns into three months. Watch for the language shift. When "explore" becomes "execute," when "might" becomes "must," when "play" becomes "produce"—the protection has failed.

You cannot optimize your way to growth. Innovation is the future. Strip out innovation headcount, strip out the future. Protect time to protect the brand's Foundations.

Six minutes at a time, the decline happens so gradually you don't notice until it's too late.

Remember, the brain's Default Mode Network—where breakthrough insights originate—is only activated during "wasted" time.

When you're doing nothing, your brain is doing everything. It's connecting disparate ideas, solving background problems, and generating the insights that will define your next decade. But only if you protect that nothing.

People solve complex problems better after periods of mind-wandering. Innovation correlates with daydreaming. Breakthrough insights emerge from boredom. The brain needs downtime to process, connect, and create.

Look at your day. Where's the boredom? Where's the mind-wandering? Where's the nothing? You've optimized it all away.

Creative teams get booked in Workfront or similar tracking tools at 85% utilization or higher. That's the target: keep everyone as close to fully utilized as possible. In reality, people are working 50 to 60 hours a week to hit that 85% number. They're at 110% capacity, chasing 85% on paper.

When do they think? When do they explore? When does the Default Mode Network activate?

It doesn't. There's no space for it. You've scheduled innovation out of existence.

The most innovative companies have the most "waste." They have people thinking about problems that don't exist yet. They have teams exploring territories with no clear destination. They have protected time that can't be colonized by urgency.

This drives the antibodies insane. They see inefficiency, underutilization, and waste. They're right. Innovation is inefficient. Discovery is wasteful. Breakthrough requires breaking things.

Real protection means real sacrifice. You're donating that time to the future, with no guarantee of return. You're funding exploration that might find nothing. You're protecting space that might stay empty.

Most leaders can't stomach this. They need to see results, measure progress, and optimize outcomes. They'd rather have 100% efficiency today than potential breakthrough tomorrow. They'd rather stay comfortable than eat the donkey.

Look at your calendar. Where's your protected time? Not "try to keep Fridays free" time. Actually protected time where innovation can happen without someone asking for the ROI.

If you can't find it, you're optimizing yourself out of a future.

Individual protection helps. But organizations need structural sanctuaries. Not conference rooms with beanbags. Actual separation that defeats the antibodies.

Physical separation. Different building. Different floor with no easy access. If you can walk there in two minutes, it's not protected. The antibodies travel through proximity. "Hey, while you're here..." is how innovation dies.

Temporal protection. Sacred time that cannot be violated. Not "we try to keep Fridays free." Inviolable blocks where efficiency is forbidden. Start with one hour a week. The same hour for everyone. No meetings scheduled. No deadlines landing. Nothing colonizing that hour. Then expand.

Cultural protection. Stories that celebrate productive failure. Metrics that measure learning, not output. Heroes who wasted time brilliantly. Most organizations celebrate efficiency, execution, and results. You need counter-mythology. The project that failed five times before succeeding. The leader who protected the mess. Time wasted that created the future.

The organization will try to colonize these sanctuaries. It will use the language of urgency, efficiency, and alignment. Compelling arguments about temporary sacrifices and getting through the quarter.

The antibodies always sound reasonable. That's why they win.

Unless you protect the space. Unless you create distance. Unless you make it inviolable.

Amazon's Lab126 created the Kindle. Apple's skunkworks created the Macintosh. Lockheed's Skunk Works developed the U-2 spy plane. The future doesn't come from making today more efficient. It comes from protecting tomorrow from today's antibodies.

19
BREAKING POINTS

Recognizing when success becomes the enemy of growth.

I was walking down the stairs of our Seattle home with my bag packed, heading to the airport for a red-eye to London. It was a Sunday evening. Earlier that day, we'd gone skiing at Snoqualmie Pass—just 59 minutes door-to-door, one of those perfect Pacific Northwest days where you can ski in the morning and be home for late lunch and a nap. Eleanor was five, and we'd just spent the day together on the magic carpet slopes, with her body pizza-slicing down the mountain, and pure joy on her face as it was the first time skiing really connected.

I'd just put her to bed. I packed my bag with the usual muscle memory of someone who'd done it hundreds of times—toiletries and power converter already in the go-bag, clothes semi-folded the efficient way that maximizes carry-on space. Walking down those stairs to catch another flight to another meeting in another time zone.

Then I stopped. And I started to cry.

Not tearing up. Not getting emotional. Full breakdown. My body stopped working. I sat on the stairs and shook like I hadn't since I was a child. My wife Joni found me there, this grown executive who'd been running global marketing campaigns, traveling the world and managing hundreds of people, crying on the stairs like a broken thing.

"What the hell is wrong with you?" she asked. She didn't sound cruel, just confused.

This wasn't who I was. I was the guy who thrived on travel, who loved the game, and who pushed through everything.

"I don't want to go," I said. "I don't want to get on the flight."

That breakdown on the stairs was my body telling me what my mind refused to admit: I had walked away from my own Foundations. The non-negotiables that made me who I am had been systematically eroded in pursuit of success at one of the world's most successful companies.

There was no exercise, no sport, and no competition—the physical challenges that had always grounded me since I was a kid running through the Australian bush.

I wasn't there for the people who mattered most, not mentally and certainly not physically. I was present in body but absent in everything that counted.

I had lost my empathy, and my sense of what made me human beyond a job title and a travel schedule.

I wasn't exploring, wasn't growing, and wasn't discovering the world the way I'd always needed to. I'd become static when my Foundation required movement.

I had to eat my own donkey.

Stop and ask yourself what you actually stand for. Not what your company values poster says. Not what you tell yourself at performance reviews. What are your Foundations? What would you never give up on? What makes you who you really are?

Be honest. Be authentic. Write it down if you need to.

Do the things you love—not because some motivational speaker told you to "follow your dreams." (I don't believe in that bullshit, because you lose the present moment chasing some fantasy future.) Do the things you love because, when you look back at your life, at what you loved as a child, at what lights you up when everything else falls away, those things reveal your Foundations.

I was a good writer. I loved words and telling stories. My entire career came from that Foundation—from being the kid who could craft a narrative, and who understood that the right words in the right order could move people. That was me. That was foundational.

However, I'd buried it under strategy decks, quarterly reviews, and global rollouts. I'd let my Principles drift so far from my Foundations that I literally broke on a staircase.

Companies do the same thing. You can push too far from what you actually are, chase too many trends, adopt too many Characteristics that look like everyone else's, and eventually something snaps. Sometimes it's catastrophic—a brand implosion, or a massive product failure. Sometimes it's quiet—a slow loss of relevance, customers who stop caring, employees who stop believing.

Your Foundations are what you come back to when everything breaks. They're what you rebuild from. And if you don't know what they are—for yourself or for your company—you're already in danger.

A smidge under six months later, I'd left Amazon. However, the breaking point stayed with me. Not the pain of it—that eventually faded. But the lesson of it. The understanding that every system, every person, and every company eventually hits the moment where what got you here won't just not get you there—it will destroy you if you keep going.

I still carry something from those years at Amazon. Not from any single terrible event, but from the accumulated pressure of trying to be someone I wasn't, of pushing past every signal my body and mind were sending, and of choosing the job over everything else until there was nothing left to choose with.

The warning signs were always there. I can tell when I'm stressed because my training stops. The cycling ends. The running disappears. The gym sessions I've built my life around—the ones that keep me centered, and that connect me back to who I am—they're the first things to go when I drift from my Foundations. They went silent at Amazon. Completely. That should have told me everything.

When you stray from your core Foundations—when you stop being you in pursuit of success—you break. Not all at once. Slowly. Like a structural beam under too much load for too long. You don't notice the microfractures until the whole thing gives way.

That's exactly how a brand breaks, too.

However, that breaking point wasn't a failure. It was information. It was my system telling me what I'd been too successful to hear—that the job had run its course. That I'd learned what I came to learn. That staying would be choosing slow death over evolution.

Every company faces these same moments. Not once, but repeatedly. What matters is whether they recognize them as transitions rather than disasters.

Amazon's Fire Phone was a breaking point—$170 million down the drain. But they learned that controlling hardware wasn't their path forward. They pivoted to Alexa and voice activation.

Tesla's production hell in 2018 was a breaking point. Musk was sleeping on the factory floor, and they were burning through cash so fast that analysts were betting on bankruptcy dates. They could have slowed down, and taken the traditional path. Instead, they powered through and emerged with capabilities no traditional manufacturer could match.

Breaking points follow the same pattern as the Explorer and Static States. Every Explorer State eventually exhausts itself. Every Static State eventually becomes unsustainable. The breaking point is the forced transition between them—the moment when you realize you can't continue as you are.

The question is whether you'll recognize what's breaking—and whether it's a Foundation you need to return to, or a Characteristic you need to let go of.

Through decades of watching companies and people break—and sometimes rebuild—I've identified three distinct types of breaking points. Each requires different responses, but all share one truth: denying them makes them worse.

Personal Breaking Points arrive when individual capacity meets organizational demand and loses. My stairs moment. The executive who realizes she hasn't seen her kids awake in two weeks. The engineer who sits in the parking lot for an hour because he can't make himself walk into the building.

Your system is telling you that the current configuration isn't sustainable. You can power through for a while—I did for months after that first breakdown. But eventually, the bill comes due. Either you choose your exit or your body chooses it for you.

Organizational Breaking Points hit when the model that created success becomes the barrier to future success. Kodak's breaking point wasn't when digital cameras appeared—it was when they realized their entire business model depended on film, while they'd invented the technology that would kill film.

These breaking points are visible in the data if you're willing to look. Not the financial data—that's a lagging indicator. The leading indicators are subtler. When your best people start leaving for "new challenges." When simple decisions require complex processes. When competitors stop competing on your terms and start competing in dimensions you don't understand.

Market Breaking Points occur when entire industries must transform. Newspapers hit one when Craigslist killed classified ads. Taxis hit one when Uber appeared. These aren't company-specific—they're ecosystem-wide forced evolutions.

The cruel irony is that the most successful companies in the old model are often the least equipped to navigate market breaking points. Their success has created antibodies against the very changes they need to make.

"You always learn more from the things that you struggled through, or things that you failed at, as opposed to the things that you did really well at."

I said this to university students recently, and I could see them writing it down, probably thinking I was talking about project failures or bad grades. But I was talking about breaking points—those moments when struggle becomes unsustainable, and forces change.

The signals are always there if you're willing to see them. Before my stairs breakdown, my body had been screaming for months. The tension headaches. The Sunday night dread. The increasing need to wind down, combined with a lack of exercise. The shorter temper with Eleanor. Each signal I ignored made the next one louder until my body simply refused to continue.

Companies are like people. They break the same way. Sometimes that breaking is good—a necessary shedding of what no longer serves them. More often, it's destructive—a slow collapse that could have been prevented if someone had been paying attention to the signals.

Organizations show the same escalating signals:

First, the talent starts leaving. Not the complainers—they never leave. The quiet stars who never complain about anything. They just quietly update their LinkedIn profiles and disappear for "personal reasons" or "new opportunities." When three of your best people leave in six months, that's a signal.

Then complexity compounds. What used to take one meeting now takes three. What used to need one approval now needs five. The organization develops scar tissue from old failures, adding process to prevent problems that no longer exist while missing the new problems emerging.

Finally, the competition shifts the game entirely. While you're optimizing your horse-drawn carriages, someone else invents the car. The breaking point isn't when they succeed—it's when you realize you can't respond without breaking everything you've built.

Breaking points are gifts.

That sounds like wellness-industry garbage, I know. But looking back at my Amazon experience, that breaking point taught me more than the success ever did. "Everyone needs to have the opportunity to work at a big company," I tell young people now. Not because big companies are wonderful—they're often brutal. But because the breaking points they create force you to confront tensions you can't learn about any other way.

Earlier in this book, I talked about Productive Discomfort—the kind that builds capability and drives growth. I also talked about the necessity of Boredom—the disciplined repetition that turns ideas into reliable systems. On the surface, these seem contradictory. How can you simultaneously embrace discomfort and boredom?

The answer is balance, and knowing which state serves your Foundation at any given moment.

Amazon taught me what I could endure. It also taught me what I shouldn't endure. Productive Discomfort stretches your capabilities. Destructive discomfort erodes your humanity. My breaking point came when I realized I'd crossed that line—when the discomfort stopped building something and started destroying something essential.

This is the paradox every company faces: Explorer State feels like the hero of business stories. It's dynamic, exciting, innovative. Static State is what actually makes companies sustainable. The trick is knowing when you've stayed in either state too long.

I'd stayed in Amazon's version of Explorer State—constant change, relentless performance pressure, perpetual transformation—until it became its own form of rigidity. I needed Static State. The grounded kind that lets you rebuild from a Foundation you can trust.

To sustain performance over time, being true to your Foundation is a necessity. And sometimes that means recognizing when the very discomfort you once needed has become the comfortable decline you need to escape.

The hardest part is that breaking points often come disguised as success. I was succeeding at Amazon by every external measure. The campaigns were working. The team was growing. The metrics were green. But inside, I was breaking. The success was actually accelerating the breakdown because it justified continuing. However, when you're winning by someone else's scorecard while losing by your own, you're not actually winning at all.

Companies need to study their breaking points in the way that archaeologists study ruins—not with shame but with curiosity. What caused this? What were the signals we missed? What capability do we need to build so this becomes a transition rather than a crisis?

Breaking points are transitions, not endings. It isn't a matter of whether you'll hit them, but whether you'll choose them or have them chosen for you.

I think about most decisions as Two-Way Doors. You can walk through, and if it doesn't work, you can walk back through and try something else. The decision is reversible. Most breaking points are Two-Way Doors pretending to be permanent. Letting go of something —a product, a strategy, a job, a way of working—is not failure. It's winning because you know when to make the transition. You're choosing to walk back through the door instead of having it slammed shut on you.

Being let go, leaving, or sunsetting something successful—none of these are failures unless there's genuine harm involved. That's the system telling you it's time to walk back through the door and try a different path.

Choose your breaking points. Break small things before you're forced to break big things. Sunset successful products while they're still profitable. Reorganize while you're still growing. Cannibalize your own business models before competitors do it for you.

Personal breaking points work the same way. You can leave the job that's separating you from your Foundations, or you can wait until your body decides for you. You can admit the model isn't working, or you can pretend until you break on a staircase. You can walk through the door yourself, or you can be pushed through it.

It took six months after leaving Amazon before I felt like myself again. Six months of what I can only describe as detox—learning to sleep without checking my phone, to have conversations without mental exit strategies, and to be present with Eleanor without calculating the opportunity cost of that time.

However, on the other side of that breaking point was everything that mattered. The clarity about what I actually valued. The understanding of my own capacity and limits. The ability to see breaking points as information rather than failure. And the wisdom to help other companies navigate their own transitions.

More importantly, I learned that breaking points aren't bugs—they're features. They're the system's way of forcing evolution when we're too comfortable, too successful, or too scared to evolve on our own. They're the universe's performance review, and the feedback is always the same: what got you here won't get you there.

Every breaking point contains the same choice: evolve or die a boring death. The kind where you slowly become irrelevant while your dashboards stay green. The kind where you optimize your way to obsolescence. The kind where you wake up one day and realize you've been dead for years, but nobody told you.

My breaking point on those stairs wasn't the end of my story. It was the beginning of understanding that every end is actually a transition.

Recognize breaking points as the price of evolution, the cost of growth, and the tuition for learning what actually matters. Break yourself before the world breaks you. Choose your transitions rather than having transitions chosen for you.

In the end, breaking points aren't really about breaking. They're about breaking through. And on the other side of every breakdown is the person or company you were meant to become—if you're brave enough to let the breaking happen.

20

FINDING YOUR FOUNDATION

The practical work of discovering what you're actually made of.

I've been thinking about that donkey meat a lot lately.

Not because I miss the taste—spoiled meat tastes like what it is, no matter how hungry you are. But because every company I've worked with, every brand I've built or rebuilt, and every CEO I've advised has eventually faced their own version of that moment in the Outback. When you face the choice between short-term discomfort and long-term success.

The moment when comfort becomes deadly. When you have to choose between eating something that makes you gag or starving to death.

Some choose to starve. They'd rather die maintaining their dignity than live by embracing discomfort. They optimize their way to irrelevance, converge toward mediocrity, and disappear so gradually that no one notices until they're gone.

Early in my advertising career, while other people pitched themselves for the sexy accounts—the glossy car brands, and the lifestyle products—I went after accounts nobody wanted. The struggling bank product. The industrial B2B division. The internal rebrand.

Why? Because those were the places where transformation was actually possible.

When you turn the worst-performing division around, people notice. When the account nobody wanted becomes the one everyone's fighting for, you've created believers. Not through manifestos, but through proof.

I've taken up golf recently, having moved to Wisconsin. I was never good at golf. In fact, I'd never played before coming here. What I love about it is the process.

You can't walk out at the beginning of summer and expect to be hitting 300-yard drives. You have to be at the range and in the studio practicing. Being good at golf means you have to play several times a week. In business, you can't expect to be innovative immediately either. Innovation is a muscle you have to use almost every single day, if not several times a week.

One of the great things about innovation and creativity and business success is you have to love the process. Being successful is not about a one-time wonder. You're not going to be great at it immediately.

You have to love the process.

⁓

Products are not Foundations. Your products will change. Your markets will shift. Your technology will evolve. If your Foundation only makes sense with your current product, you've confused strategy with identity.

Michelin makes tires, but they're in the mobility business. Amazon started with books, but they're in the business of removing friction. Apple makes devices, but they're in the business of making technology feel human.

What business are you really in?

If you can't answer that question without naming your product, you haven't found your Foundation yet. Keep digging.

Every company faces their donkey meat moment. Not once, but

repeatedly. Sometimes monthly, sometimes yearly, but always eventually.

You may be facing it right now.

Maybe your industry is converging, and everyone's starting to look the same. Maybe you've been optimizing the same model for five years. Maybe your best people are leaving because they're bored. Maybe you know, deep in your gut, that comfort is killing you but you don't know how to choose discomfort.

When I don't know what to do, I start with one question: what's actually frustrating customers?

Not where can we make money. Where are people genuinely frustrated? CarMax figured out that people hated haggling over car prices more than they cared about getting the absolute lowest price. That single insight built the entire company. Frustration is energy. People will change their behavior and pay money to make frustration disappear.

Then I write from the customer's perspective. Actually write as them. "I need..." not "Customers want..." When I rewrote that failed Amazon document from a seller's point of view instead of Amazon's, everything changed. I stopped writing about what we could build and started writing about what they needed.

Work backward from the perfect end state. What would the ideal customer experience look like? Start there. Figure out what's required to deliver that.

Kill anything that compromises your Foundation for short-term revenue. If you can't explain how something helps customers without mentioning your company's benefits, you're building the wrong thing.

Measure what customers get, not what you get. Don't pitch "$10M in revenue." Pitch "saves customers 10 hours per month." Revenue follows if customer value is real. You can't manage revenue—you can only report it after it happens. But you can manage how many customer problems you solve, how many experiments you run, and how often you listen rather than assume.

The numbers take care of themselves when you get this right.

If you care about shareholder value for even a second, you're forgetting about the customer. And that's how companies die—watching the wrong scorecard while the game changes around them.

The brand demand score matters more than the S&P 500. The net promoter score matters more than your stock price. What customers would miss if you disappeared matters more than what analysts predict you'll earn.

CVS walked away from $2 billion in cigarette sales because selling cancer sticks violated their promise of helping people on their path to better health.

Patagonia gave away the entire company—$3 billion—because their Foundation is saving the planet, not making money from it.

Southwest still doesn't charge for bags, leaving $800 million on the table annually, because their Foundation is democratic air travel, and taxes on traveling shouldn't exist.

These aren't marketing decisions. They're Foundation tests. And Foundations, real Foundations, are expensive by design. If your Principles don't cost you anything, they're not Principles—they're preferences.

The choice isn't really about comfort versus discomfort. It's about meaning versus meaninglessness. Purpose versus profit. Creating versus extracting.

To be extraordinary is not about ease. It's about meaning something to customers, not the stock market.

Discomfort is not a dirty word. Yet many think it is.

Every company has eaten donkey meat at some point. Inside every company, there is rotten flesh that needs to be uncomfortably gotten rid of. Every company and CEO has their own donkey meat moment. It penetrates deep into the organization, and you have to work out what to do. You have to decide: short-term or long-term?

Someone high up once told me I have "the biggest gut in the business." I took offense at the time. Now I understand it as the highest compliment.

Gut equals listen—I watch and listen a lot.

That gut was formed at seven years old, watching my parents choose exploration over comfort, even when exploration meant eating donkey. It was refined at Amazon, where Bezos taught me you don't need 100% of facts, just 70% and the courage to act. It was tested at Nike, Airbnb, LVMH, Microsoft, Verizon, and other places where I learned that every great brand has the same choice: conform or create, optimize or explore, and live comfortably or live meaningfully.

I've made my choice. I'll eat the donkey every time. Not because I like the taste, but because I like who I become when I'm willing to eat it. I like the companies it builds. I like the people it attracts. I like the impossible it makes possible.

This book began with spoiled donkey meat in the Australian Outback and ends with a simple question:

What's your donkey?

What's the uncomfortable truth you're avoiding? The difficult decision you're postponing? The transformation you know you need but haven't started? The Foundation you claim to have but won't defend?

Find it. Name it. Then eat it.

Not because anyone's making you. Not because it's strategic. But because, on the other side of that discomfort is the only thing that matters: becoming who you're supposed to be instead of who you're settling for.

The world doesn't need another company that does what everyone else does, slightly better, slightly cheaper, and slightly faster.

The world needs companies with the courage to be terrible at some things so they can be extraordinary at what matters.

Companies willing to take a point of view that pisses off some people.

Companies that would rather fail at something new than succeed at something stale.

Companies that understand their Foundation so deeply that hard decisions become easy.

Companies willing to eat the donkey.

Here's the final truth, the one that took me from the Outback to the boardroom to understand: the donkey is the test, not the enemy. It's the universe asking: do you want this enough? Do you believe in your Foundation enough? Are you willing to pay the price for being extraordinary?

Most companies say yes but their actions say no. They want the results of exploration without the discomfort. They want the Foundation without the cost. They want to matter without sacrifice.

It doesn't work that way. It never has.

Your Foundation is permanent. Your states are temporary. Your products will change. But who you are—what you stand for, what you're willing to suffer for, and what you'd protect even if it cost you everything—that's your cast iron Foundation.

Find yours. Defend it. Build everything else on top of it.

EPILOGUE

The Return Home

In the Australian summer of 2025, my wife, our eleven-year-old daughter, and I flew back to the place where everything began. On paper, it was a family holiday. In reality, it was something deeper—something I had been avoiding for years. It was about making peace with my parents, with my country, and, more honestly, with myself.

My parents are in their late eighties now. They've lived many lives inside one. I knew, as the plane touched down in Sydney, that this trip would probably be the last time I would see them alive. That kind of truth sits heavily on a person. There's no excitement in it—just a quiet ache. Returning to the place that was your Foundation is strange. It's familiar and foreign at the same time. It holds who you were and reminds you of who you've become.

We did the usual things: the tourist spots in Sydney, family dinners, and visiting cousins on a farm outside Melbourne—sheep, horses, dust, and all the noise of a life I had once lived. Then we flew north, up into FNQ—Far North Queensland—where the heat and humidity wrap around you like a memory you didn't ask to feel.

The moment we stepped off the plane, it hit me. The smell of the

Daintree Forest. The damp tropical air. The screeching cicadas. The winding roads through the rainforest. And that heat—the unrelenting, shoulder-heavy heat. It all came rushing back. I was home. I was back in my element. Back to my Foundations.

We didn't retrace the rugged routes of my childhood this time. We stayed in a hotel in Port Douglas, went out to the reef, and found ourselves swimming in four-foot seas until the boat crew called us in for safety. Our daughter—eleven years old, fearless, and wrapped in a stinger suit—swam through hundreds of jellyfish above the Great Barrier Reef in the middle of the ocean with no land in sight. It was surreal. And symbolic. We were all navigating through unknown water, trusting ourselves to float.

But the real story of this trip wasn't the reef, the heat, or even my parents. It was the reconciliation with who I had become.

If I hadn't left Australia twenty years ago, would I have the life I have now? Would I have met my wife and traveled countless miles together? For she is the one who understands me the most. Would we have the daughter we have now? Would I have seen the world I've seen, stood in boardrooms I never belonged in, or stood on podiums I never imagined I could? I have been hired, fired, lifted, dropped, praised, criticized, and wrong more times than I can count. I have made mistakes—many of which I am deeply sorry for. But I've grown.

I've learned that the power of me—and the power of any company —is never about the individual hero. It's about a team's inputs. Associates working in unison. A shared rhythm. A shared Foundation. Australia reminded me of that. Watching our daughter hold a rhinoceros beetle the size of her hand. Seeing crocodile warning signs on the riverbanks. Feeling the raw, ugly beauty of nature that shaped me.

Then, in a small art shop in Cairns, a First Nations painter from the Northern Tablelands, Kelly Barclay, took the time—real time—to walk our daughter through her art. She explained Dreamtime. Ochre. Color. Family. Land. She explained how stories live longer than people do. I remember her warmth, her pride, and the simplicity of her truth. That one encounter changed something in me. It anchored me again.

And that brings me to you. Because this book was never really about me. It was about you. Your company. Your team. Your future. Your Foundations.

Three questions to ask yourself before you put this book down:

Are you in a growth state or static? Not your title. Not your salary. You. Are you stretching? Uncomfortable? Doing the hard, unglamorous work that actually makes you better? Or have you settled into comfortable decline?

Is your company growing or static? Strip away the excuses— tariffs, politics, budgets, headcount, or market cycles. Beneath the noise, is your organization leaning forward or leaning back? Are your Foundations clear and lived? Or laminated and forgotten on a conference room wall?

Twenty years from now, would you be proud of what you're building today? If the answer is no, that's your starting point. Work backward from there. Build the life and company that future-you would actually admire.

Growth comes from Foundations. Foundations create clarity. Clarity gives direction. Direction builds momentum.

Everything else is noise.

You'll have to do hard things. Face uncomfortable truths. Disappoint people. Be misunderstood. Stand alone sometimes. Eat donkey.

You'll be better for it. Your team will be better for it. Your company will be better for it.

Growth isn't a reward. It's what happens when you refuse to stay static.

Look at your Foundations. Your real ones, not the ones printed on a wall.

Will you grow? Or will you drift?

The next chapter starts the moment you choose.

ACKNOWLEDGMENTS

This book exists because a small group of people had far more patience with me than they ever should have.

To those who guided me directly, challenged my thinking, and kept me as straight as possible when it would have been easier to let me wander. You didn't soften the edges. You sharpened them. You told me what I needed to hear, not what was comfortable. This work carries your fingerprints whether you know it or not.

To the people I've raced with and raced against in Ironman and ultras. You taught me what endurance really is. Long before it became a business metaphor, it was a lived experience. Quiet mornings. Heavy legs. Honest effort. Shared suffering and silent respect. You showed me that growth rarely looks heroic while it's happening.

To my home country. The place that taught me resilience before I had language for it. Where distance, heat, and isolation make comfort optional and foundations non negotiable. The Outback doesn't care who you think you are. It only responds to what you can endure and what you're willing to carry.

And most of all, to my wife.

We met when my days started before light. I would leave while the world slept to train, to think, to push. I would return changed in small, incremental ways. You let me grow. You let me become who I am. You never tried to shape me into something safer or smaller. And when I needed it, you gave me the look. The one that cuts through ego and brings me back to what matters.

This book is as much yours as it is mine.

And to Eleanor. You will always be my little girl. No matter how tall you grow or how far you go. Everything I do is, in some way, about leaving you something solid to stand on. I will live for you. I will protect you. Always.